Praise for Superpower Europe

'Marc De Vos outlines vividly the crossroads in history at which Europe finds itself and the major challenges that lie ahead.'

Alexander De Croo, Prime Minister of Belgium

'Marc De Vos walks us through the growing pains of a Europe randomly but rapidly developing into a real Union, each solution leading to more problems. If EU politics needs focus, *Superpower Europe* points the way forward.'

Guy Verhofstadt, President of European Movement International, MEP and former prime minister of Belgium

'A lucid and convincing analysis of Europe's necessary response to the new world disorder. De Vos sees a new European Union emerging, defined by geostrategic choices, power politics, and state capitalism.'

Luuk van Middelaar, Author of *Pandemonium: Saving Europe* and founder of the Brussels Institute for Geopolitics

'Reflection on the future of Europe is needed more than ever. As always, Marc De Vos colours and enriches the debate with his insights.'

Johan Van Overtveldt, Member of the European Parliament and former Belgian finance minister

'This book is important and insightful. Read it! Europe is at a crossroads in a fast-changing world. The proposals here for a multi-layered, defence-oriented, democratic, stronger and larger EU are compelling – and the UK must be part of it.'

Sir Nick Harvey, former UK Defence Minister and CEO of the European Movement (UK)

Superpower Europe

Superpower Europe

The European Union's
Silent Revolution

MARC DE VOS

polity

ISBN-13: 978-1-5095-6525-2
ISBN-13: 978-1-5095-6526-9(pb)

A catalogue record for this book is available from the British Library.

Library of Congress Control Number: 2024901809

Typeset in 11 on 14pt Warnock Pro
by Cheshire Typesetting Ltd, Cuddington, Cheshire
Printed and bound in Great Britain by TJ Books Ltd, Padstow, Cornwall

The publisher has used its best endeavours to ensure that the URLs for external websites referred to in this book are correct and active at the time of going to press. However, the publisher has no responsibility for the websites and can make no guarantee that a site will remain live or that the content is or will remain appropriate.

Every effort has been made to trace all copyright holders, but if any have been overlooked the publisher will be pleased to include any necessary credits in any subsequent reprint or edition.

For further information on Polity, visit our website:
politybooks.com

Contents

Abbreviations

ACI	Anti-Coercion Instrument
AI	artificial intelligence
CBAM	Carbon Border Adjustment Mechanism
CCS	carbon capture and storage
CFIUS	Committee on Foreign Investment in the United States
CHIPS and Science Act	Creating Helpful Incentives to Produce Semiconductors (CHIPS) and Science Act
CRMA	Critical Raw Materials Act
ECB	European Central Bank
ECSC	European Coal and Steel Community
EDF	European Defence Fund
EIB	European Investment Bank
EPF	European Peace Facility
ESA	European Space Agency
EU	European Union
Euratom	European Atomic Energy Community
FIRRMA	Foreign Investment Risk Review Modernization Act
IMF	International Monetary Fund

IPCEI	Important Projects of Common European Interest
NATO	North Atlantic Treaty Organization
NDAA	National Defense Authorization Act
NZIA	Net-Zero Industry Act
OECD	Organisation for Economic Co-operation and Development
TEU	Treaty on European Union
TTC	Trade and Technology Council
UN	United Nations
USA	United States of America
WTO	World Trade Organization

Introduction:
Silent Revolution in Europe

The European Union (EU) is a behemoth, composed of twenty-seven member states and 450 million inhabitants. It is the third largest economic power, and its member states, collectively, have the third largest defence budget on earth, after the United States (USA) and China. It has twelve countries (totalling 146 million inhabitants) on the official waiting list to join and more than sixty additional countries worldwide enjoy privileged economic and political relations with it, regionally and bilaterally. No other coalition of nation-states in the world approaches the EU in scope, depth or impact. No country in the world can afford to ignore the EU in the face of the great political, economic and environmental challenges of our time.

The average European supports Europe but is ambivalent about the EU.[1] The EU is perceived by many as a playground full of insiders and pundits. Apart from the odd Brussels summit covered in the media, the EU is typically viewed as an abstraction, far removed from the day-to-day concerns of European citizens and portrayed as a scapegoat or even a tyrant by certain political or media groups. Outside Europe, the EU is equally misunderstood and underestimated. Its façade masks a complex ballet of senior officials choreographed by national politicians. As the late Henry Kissinger once quipped, 'Who do I call if I want to speak to Europe?'.

Yet the anonymous, underestimated and misunderstood EU is experiencing something of a heyday. The climate crisis, the pandemic, the war in Ukraine, the end of globalization and the emerging cold war with China have made the EU by far the most important political force in Europe. The extent of the crisis management required in recent times has not only mobilized the EU; it has also transformed it. We live in a time of European revolution. As the world order has been tilting, so have the EU's mission and position. This book documents the EU's ongoing metamorphosis: from a European community to a geostrategic coalition of Eurasian countries, from a union of values to a union of power, and from a market project to a state project.

Europe is quietly moving towards federal superpower status in a new world order. This book points out the profound implications of this, not only for the functioning of the EU itself, but also for its relations with its member states – and the relations among those member states themselves – for its relations with third countries and for its transatlantic and international relations. No one can afford to ignore, disregard or underestimate the EU any longer.

The transmutation of the EU is following at speed on the back of wave after wave of successive crises, advancing at every turn of crisis policy, driven by elite politics and Eurocrats, yet with no great public or democratic symbolic moment. Largely unnoticed by the general public, the EU is undergoing a historic transformation. And this transformation, this book argues, is as desirable as it is inevitable and necessary. However, the new EU needs to resolve a number of tensions: between values and interests, between geography and geopolitics, between democracy and technocracy, between market and state, and between EU member states themselves.

In today's changing Europe, we see the contours of the EU becoming increasingly similar to those of the USA. The new EU shares with the USA a geopolitical, industrial, technological and defence mission that is tailored to a new world order characterized by superpower conflict. In this, Brussels is Europe's Washington, DC. It is the new EU that sets the beat in Europe, just as the federal government determines the national agenda in the USA. But this evolution in political fact needs to be embedded in the EU's institutional norms and structures. It is an evolution that is changing the identity and the balance of the EU itself, requiring a new understanding among its member states. The EU must rediscover and redefine itself in a way that makes sense not only to its member states but also to the rest of the world if it is to avoid a crisis of legitimacy. To that process, this book aims to contribute.[2]

1

Fault Lines

The Poster Child of Globalization

As the European continent experiences its first war of aggression in seventy-five years, as the USA and China wage a new cold war of great power rivalry, as an enlarged North Atlantic Treaty Organization (NATO) rediscovers itself, as the entire planet experiences a climate crisis and as the European common market celebrates its thirtieth anniversary amid an energy crisis and transition, it is a good time to reflect on the future of the EU.

Europe, the so-called European project, the European unification that started just after the Second World War and eventually became the EU, has been both a passion and a career for me. I am a big *believer*. I came of age with a Europe that itself came to maturity after the fall of Communism, unifying its war-torn member countries in a project of freedom and openness, and standing side by side with the USA as the architect and inspiration of a free and prosperous world order. As an academic, policy expert, consultant and public intellectual, I have contributed to and commented on the European legal order on which the EU was founded.

That EU is today being buffeted by new historical forces. Founding father Jean Monnet's oft-used motto '*l'Europe se fera dans les crises et elle sera la somme des solutions apportées à ces crises* [Europe will be made in crises and will be the sum of the solutions applied to those crises]' has once again proved its worth. I would venture as far as to say that these days the EU is being not only shaped but fundamentally transformed by crisis; we are experiencing a revolution in the EU, albeit one that is going largely unnoticed by those outside it.

Europe or the EU – I am deliberately going to use those terms interchangeably to respond to the *Schwung* [momentum] of our times – is an answer to two questions:

- How do we as Europeans want to interact within Europe?
- How do we as Europeans want to interact with the world outside Europe?

For a long time, the EU had to deal mainly with the first question. The answer to the second question was considered an extension of the answer to the first.

Within Europe, the EU was the exponent of first a Western coalition and second – after the implosion of the Soviet Union – a broader globalization that in each case rested on the same pillars outside Europe: trade, treaties, rules, freedoms. There was a close strategic synergy between internal European unification and external international priorities that we could leave to the USA or to international institutions such as the United Nations (UN), the World Trade Organization (WTO) and the International Monetary Fund (IMF).

In other words, internal European political unification long ran parallel to the external geopolitical realities of Europe. In the heyday of globalization, around the late twentieth/early twenty-first century, the EU was even seen as a role model. Nowhere in the world had sovereign nation-states gone further in opening borders and markets, in facilitating the free movement of people, business and capital, in separating markets from governments in building prosperity on free trade, and all regulated by common norms and overseen by common institutions. The EU was internally institutionalized globalization of a higher state order, and thus externally a global reference.

But all that has changed dramatically in a very short space of time. In recent years, the EU increasingly has had to deal with the second aforementioned question – of how we as Europeans want to interact with the world outside Europe – in a world where globalization has been dismantled at breakneck speed. The banking crisis and the euro crisis, the refugee crisis, Brexit, the pandemic, the climate crisis, the war in Ukraine and the global rivalry between America and China: this is the new environment in which the EU has to re-answer the old questions.

At Odds with the World

This new environment represents a strategic shift for the EU; it has revolutionized the way the EU thinks and acts.[1] The model of the EU as a political project and the geopolitical world outside the EU are no longer in synergy; they are in opposition. No longer a model for the world, the EU of the present time is at odds with and threatened by the world. The old EU, which was based on cooperation, connection, open borders, free trade and free movement of people, business and capital, is having to adjust to a new world order that runs on rivalry, conflict, autonomy, protectionism and nationalism.

At the same time, Europe's relative weight in the world has shrunk – economically, demographically, culturally and geopolitically. Our problems also used to be the world's problems because, together with the USA, we dominated internationally. Our Western norms and values in relation to democracy and human rights used to be the gold standard. Our solutions inspired the rest of the world because our economies and societies were considered superior. Now, increasingly, the world's problems are also our problems because the world has become more important to us than we are to the world. Now our norms and values are contested because major countries like China, Russia, India and South Africa are pursuing their own models of civilization and rejecting ours as imperialist or hypocritical, while many developing countries want to reduce 'Western influence' and posit their values as equal.[2] Now the world's solutions are increasingly our threats because they are at odds with our values, norms and interests. Just look at how the current war in Europe is being viewed outside our continent and North America, not through a European or Western lens, but through an alternative – neutral or even Russia-friendly – international lens, and how this is hindering us in our war aims and strategy, especially when it comes to mobilizing countries in a sanctions regime against Russia.[3] Look at how the so-called BRICS grouping of countries – Brazil, Russia, India, China and South Africa – has evolved from a club for growth and investment to an alternative G7: a geopolitical alliance that is challenging the current world order, which is perceived as Western, and being courted by upstart countries that want to join for precisely that reason.[4]

The primary question is how we in Europe want to deal with this strategic shift. The secondary question is what role we want to assign to the EU – which, until further notice, remains an alliance of sovereign European nation-states – or to the member states themselves.

I identify three axes in the transformation of Europe and of the EU:

- The EU is becoming a closed geostrategic project – rather than an open community of like-minded nations.
- The EU is becoming a superpower project – rather than a postmodern peace project.

- The EU is becoming a state project – rather than a free-market project.

These three axes are still in formation, while the transformation of the EU is continuing apace.[5] I outline them in this book as trends, looking back at recent developments and looking ahead to their logical continuation and extrapolation. They have fundamental consequences: for the EU itself, for the position of the member states in the EU, for the relations between those member states, for the position of the EU in the world, for the alliance between Europe and the USA, and for anyone who wants to understand the ecosystem of and around the EU. That is the focus of this book. Need it be said that I use a broad brush, that I formulate only my personal vision, and take the balcony view?

2

A Geostrategic Project

A European Community of Values

Europe is, of course, a continent, but the EU has long been an open political project with no geographical predestination. European unification after the Second World War evolved not as a matter of geographical 'manifest destiny', as happened in nineteenth-century America, but rather as a matter of cultural-communitarian 'manifest history', sporadically with some gentle coercion from a USA that was fearful of nationalism and eager for stability in Europe.

The Europe of patriarch Jean Monnet was a kind of post-war Western European fraternity that grew up around hereditary enemies France and Germany, before being rather inevitably joined by a democratizing Southern Europe. The accession of the United Kingdom was special, precisely because of the special position of the British Isles in the history of Western Europe, but it was also logical and for the same reason. Indeed, Brexit is the flip side of this history. Not coincidentally, European integration in this phase happened under the official rubric of a European 'Community' – expressing ties of history that form a common bond and underlie the unification of common national interests – though of course it was also a community that, from an American perspective, responded to a harsh cold-war logic of regional blocs and anti-communism, particularly in the case of the United Kingdom.

After the fall of Communism, the same European-communitarian logic applied to the enlargement of the EU in 2004 and 2007 to include the former Eastern Bloc and the Soviet countries and states of the Czech Republic, Estonia, Hungary, Latvia, Lithuania, Poland, Slovakia, Slovenia, Bulgaria and Romania. Behold culturally and historically European countries that had simply ended up on the wrong side of the Iron Curtain, combined with a West and an East Germany that were destined for reunification. This did bring some initial immigration concerns of a mainly economic nature, and it did fall quite a bit short in the subsequent cultural praxis of democracy and rule of law – think of the vicissitudes with populism and 'illiberal democracy' in Hungary and Poland or with corruption in Romania – but it never encountered any real geostrategic objections. Of course, the 'Europeanization' of former Eastern Bloc and Soviet countries was the result of the geopolitical landslide caused by the implosion of the Soviet Union. But their entry into the EU was much less a matter of geopolitics than their entry into NATO.

Before the end of the Cold War, EU enlargement – in terms of both its membership and its geography – was primarily an internal European mission. This remained the case at the end of the Cold War, when a sense of European mission and destiny trumped any geostrategic considerations. The EU was to the European continent what globalization was to the whole world: an ever bigger and more inclusive home for a growing community of nation-states with a core of common values and a common market. The EU saw itself as a 'union among the peoples of Europe', united by common values of freedom, democracy, rule of law, human rights, pluralism and non-discrimination.[1]

Tellingly, to this day the official criteria for joining the EU focus on stable democratic institutions and a functioning market economy, ignoring any formal limitations of geography or cultural identity.[2] These so-called Copenhagen criteria date from the 1990s. At that time, both Europe and the wider Western world cherished the belief that economic and political freedom would spontaneously converge and unite humanity, as we shall see. The EU could therefore continue its march eastward, blissfully unconcerned about its internal cohesion or the effects of its enlargement on the rest of the Eurasian continent. The EU was an open space, not a geographical place.[3]

That position has been totally reversed. The pendulum has swung from world order to world disorder, triggered by the global power conflict between the USA and China, and recuperated and exacerbated on our continent by an atavistic, revisionist, jingoistic and militaristic Russia.[4]

The second existential question – relating to how Europe wants to deal with the (more dangerous) world – is forcing the contemporary EU to consciously position itself geostrategically. While EU enlargement started off as an external dynamic aimed at broadening European community building, now it is the opposite: enlargement is an internal European question about the EU's strategic-geographical position in the world.

In other words, the very existence of the EU and its composition are matters of institutionalized geopolitical strategy in a changing world order. Either we define that strategy ourselves or it is projected onto us by the outside world. This means that the EU must very consciously address these questions: where are my borders, where is my sphere of influence? By asking these questions, we think about Europe's position on the vast Eurasian continent in terms that are analogous to how Putin and his Russia think about it: as a projection of our international strategic position, rather than as a common expression of values and identity. We do not have to fall into an existential geographical obsession like Russia; we do not necessarily need

to construct our spatial footprint as an offensive threat to the
outside world; but we do need to embrace and answer the
question of our geostrategic position.

The case of Turkey is a telling example of open European
unification without a European strategic-geographical identity. Turkey's pathway to EU membership started under a Cold
War logic in the early 1960s, complementing its earlier NATO
membership. It agreed a customs union with the EU in 1995,
which was reconfirmed under the aforementioned Copenhagen
criteria in the early twenty-first century.[5] Meanwhile, however,
European geographical history is back and Turkey as a member
state seems a mistake or a utopia, at least for now. At the same
time, Moldova, Albania, Serbia and Ukraine, among others,
have also become candidate countries for EU membership,
reflecting an EU expansion that is now primarily geostrategic,
not Euro-communitarian. Whipped up by Russian aggression and in the context of the new world order, the EU is
becoming less a values-driven European club and more a geopolitical coalition on the western part of Eurasia. The eastern
ring of (potential) EU member states with mostly Slavic and/
or Orthodox cultural-historical roots – think Albania, Bosnia
and Herzegovina, Montenegro, northern Macedonia, Serbia
and later Ukraine – testifies to an EU that is no longer primarily a community of historically European nations. Moreover,
since Brexit, the EU's western external border has become less
Atlantic and its centre of gravity has clearly shifted eastwards
towards Central and Eastern Europe.

A Geostrategic Coalition

Enlarging the EU is a slow bureaucratic process with its fair
share of transitory bumps and subsequent bruises, as evidenced by the struggles with recent acquisitions such as, say,
Hungary and Poland. On average, the accession process for

a new member state takes more than nine years from the time of formal application, which is often preceded by years of diplomatic, institutional and legislative preparation.[6] If we in Europe want to establish our own geographical sphere of influence, and not simply undergo, defensively or reactively, what the outside world unleashes on us, the EU will have to show creativity in turning its geostrategic moment into real momentum. Thus, EU enlargement must not remain a merely passive process, with eager and suitable candidates spontaneously falling into the European fold; it must also become a strategic process that proactively pushes and pulls wavering countries into the European orbit on the basis of conscious European strategic geographical positioning.

Devising a layered or tiered membership that separates economic integration from political integration has long been under consideration as a conduit for expansive European unification overall. The EU has long been experimenting with various and flexible degrees of integration. For instance, currently the eurozone is limited to twenty of the twenty-seven EU member states. Further, through association treaties, the Euro–Mediterranean Partnership and the Eastern Partnership, the EU has developed relationships of preferential cooperation and selective integration with more than twenty of its neighbouring non-member countries. The opt-out clause technique – (in)famously obtained and favoured by the United Kingdom pre-Brexit – can allow EU member states to be on the sidelines of EU initiatives they do not support. The European Economic Area extends the European single market to third countries Iceland, Liechtenstein and Norway. And so on.

The strategic consideration in any geographical expansion of the EU has invariably been: is it broadening or deepening first? Should the EU grow in geographical scope and number of member states first, or deepen the integration of EU powers and policies first? We can obviously do both at the same time, if we work in layers: a deepened proto-federal core EU – a coalition of the daring and the willing that should evidently include at least a hard core of historical member states and a cluster of the larger countries – and an expanded looser layer around it.[7] Moreover, widening is the new deepening: deepening towards a geostrategic EU works precisely through geographical widening because geographical enlargement is the gateway to the EU's new geostrategic role.

Geographical extension of the EU to include new member states thus becomes the means by which the EU can strategically deepen its mission and its policies: the two cannot exist without each other. The EU can only truly assume a geostrategic role by reaffirming itself geographically. An EU that stands for European security, protection and autonomy in a hostile world order is an EU that must be able to build on strategic territorial integrity. Geopolitics translated into geography becomes the main prism for demarcating the borders of the EU. In other words, EU membership, whatever its possible layers or gradations, becomes a geographical expression of geopolitics rather than of democracy, trade or identity.

The old, values-driven EU asked itself who it was; the new, geostrategic EU is asking itself where it should be. By definition, the answer implies a broader geographical footprint. European geostrategy in today's dangerous world order requires greater European reach vis-à-vis the geopolitical opportunists, waverers and fence-sitters among the neighbouring countries who will otherwise cause strategic friction and risks in Europe. In this new context, we can look at, say, the Balkans or Turkey from a different perspective. The EU will want to prevent Turkey from continuing to bet on multiple horses just as it will want to prevent Russia from fomenting unrest in the Balkans. Perhaps a historical bridge country like Turkey, astride Europe and Asia, might fit in as a (partial) member state of a (layered) geostrategic EU, while it hardly fits in as a full-blooded member state of the EU as a values-based community of historically European nations. If the old EU struggled to determine if

Turkey was a European country, Turkey would now have to give up its neo-Ottoman aspirations for the sake of the new geostrategic EU. This is how we can redraw the geopolitical map of Europe in our favour. And perhaps the British will fit into such a set-up as well, in time.

Seeking to build a tiered and/or widened EU with Eurasian components is becoming easier and more necessary as Ukraine – officially recognized as a candidate country by the EU since 23 June 2022 – is turbo-charging the EU's geographical expansion, with a palette of possible membership layers. A layered EU maximizes Europe's geostrategic weight in the world; throughout and after the war, Ukraine belongs in the EU's geostrategic footprint. However, the example of Turkey shows that an intention of membership and effective membership can be two different things, on both sides. Ukraine is a vast and poor country that culturally is both European and Slavic-Orthodox; it has a large agricultural sector and old industry, a legacy of corruption, and is in need of huge amounts of reconstruction, defence and security aid. A 'normal' process towards EU membership, with ripple-free integration into the economic, political, environmental and rules-driven EU, with an inevitable adjustment of the budget planning and funding flows in the EU itself, would take an agonizingly long time, unbearably long for what is the dominant reason for Ukrainian membership: geopolitics. If Europe is really serious about accepting Ukraine into its membership, it seems that candidate country Ukraine will be the proverbial tail wagging the dog, requiring the EU to adapt to the candidate country as well.

To be properly geostrategic, the EU must also be institutionally flexible. As the institutional expression of the European sphere of influence, the EU must be able to handle variations and degrees of European integration in line with a greater diversity of member states. Full membership may be unthinkable for the post-Brexit United Kingdom, for example, but British–European integration for, say, cyber security, migration control and critical supply chains seems unavoidable. Such strategic flexibility is what the EU of the future must be able to offer and to cope with.

A Eurasian Union?

At the same time, we have to realize what a geostrategic reality implies. A geostrategic EU draws countries into the European sphere that would not otherwise belong there. If we want Ukraine to be European, regardless of its final formal status in the EU, we have to realize what that will require when Russia considers Ukraine to be integral to the Russian sphere – historically, culturally, geographically and strategically. If we want countries like Moldova, Albania or Serbia in the European sphere, we must evolve the EU's membership palette into much more than a combination of markets, sustainability, democracy and money. Compared to the old EU, future EU membership or some variant thereof may mean less in terms of economy, ecology and democracy, but certainly more in other, more geopolitical and strategic domains of new European integration.

More than in the past, geostrategy means an EU in which the binding agent lies in geographical and strategic interests rather than in common values or in a manifest European cultural-historical identity, and in which the logic and the function of EU membership are directed towards a hostile outside world. This creates a new value proposition for the EU, in line with its broader transition towards becoming a power union, which we discuss in chapter 3.

A geostrategic EU also affects the world outside it. It forces countries outside the EU to adopt their own compensatory positioning. In Russia's case, this includes aligning with China and trading with India, while engaging in hot or cold war with Europe. For the USA, the relationship between a geostrategic EU and Russia is part of its superpower relationship with China, and vice versa for China. A geostrategic EU has knock-on effects. Vis-à-vis friend and foe alike, it blurs the distinctions between economics, politics, security and defence. A geostrategic EU both reflects and accelerates the evolution towards a new multipolar world order that, in turn, confronts European countries with challenges that can only be solved with European geopolitics and strategy. Geostrategy implies for the EU a switch from being a subject to being an author of the world order. It implies consequences outside Europe with mutually reinforcing second-round strategic effects for the EU itself.

A geostrategic Europe is almost unthinkable without the EU as the current home of economic, technological and political integration in Europe. The impetus for that evolution has already been given. In the autumn of 2022, the European Political Community was established as an intergovernmental forum with continental aspirations following Russia's invasion of Ukraine. Its objective is distinctly geopolitical and geostrategic. It combines all EU member states, all candidate countries including Turkey and Ukraine, other European countries such as the United Kingdom and Switzerland, as well as more peripheral countries such as Armenia, Azerbaijan and Georgia, for common interests including security, stability, prosperity and energy security.[8] The focus is on interests rather than values, on cooperation rather than rules.

Flexible, inclusive and informal in set-up, and geographically simultaneously pan-European and partly Eurasian, the European Political Community offers a convenient alternative, or a useful complement, to the unwieldy, exclusive and formal EU itself. A wartime child will have to grow up in peacetime, summitry will have to produce action, international and institutional relations will evolve, but the very existence of the European Political Community points the way to European geostrategic integration.[9] It demonstrates the underlying transformation in crucial EU member states: in France, which no longer rejects further enlargement of the EU and no longer considers NATO brain-dead; in Germany, which no longer accommodates the Putin regime and instead calls for a veritable *Zeitenwende* or epochal shift; and in Italy, which no longer covets China and its New Silk Road with China-subservient trading partners.

We are awake. We realize that the EU must become the centre of gravity of a geostrategic Europe; that the logic and the configuration of the EU must change. A broader geography, with a variety of membership formulas, with varying degrees of integration and cooperation, is a necessary precondition if the EU is to continue to provide for our security and prosperity on the Eurasian continent. But it is not a sufficient condition. Geography is only a stepping stone to enable the new EU to function as a true power union.

3

A Superpower Project

The End of Globalization

The EU is economically a giant, politically a dwarf and militarily a worm, according to another popular saying. European political integration began as a peace project, with NATO and the USA providing our security. Europe's strength was also its weakness: the EU was built on the soft power of democracy, human rights, humanitarian values, on free trade and prosperity crowned with access to or membership of that giant European market. After the fall of Communism and the 'end of history',[1] these 'soft values' were in vogue globally. For a brief moment, liberalism, the societal model with which the Free West had won the Cold War, was ostensibly the last surviving '-ism'. That had major consequences.

Ideologically, so-called neoliberalism shifted the centre of politics towards more free markets, more free trade and less government intervention in the economy.[2] Culturally and socially, the conviction of a shared human identity and destiny emerged. More economic freedom, more growth and more prosperity were expected to bring more political freedom, greater individualism and more human rights everywhere.[3]

Ensure that poor countries grow a middle class and you ensure worldwide democracy and peace. Technocratically, a real policy menu was available to pull this off: the so-called Washington Consensus. The IMF, the World Bank and the US government agreed on growth-enhancing policy priorities for developing countries, including privatization, liberalization and free trade.[4]

All of this came together in, and paved the way for, globalization: the global dismantling of borders; the liberalization of trade, money flows and national currencies; the promotion of international mobility, transnational education and cultural exchange. Economic globalization rested on a postmodern phase in the history of nation-states, where states voluntarily gave up a degree of national sovereignty to an international legal order based on security and prosperity, on cooperation and interdependence.[5] In this respect, the EU was globalization on steroids, a kind of regional super-globalization that was ever-expanding, increasingly inspiring and even considered a global reference.[6]

In that world, the main European contributions to geopolitics were the lure and the example of a rich, large common market combined with free democratic societies, through membership, association agreements and trade deals. The prospect of EU membership would suck entire countries into a transformational journey involving national implementation of thousands of pages of European legislation. The magnetism of the European single market – the crowning achievement of intra-European 'globalization' – strengthened old EU member states' belief that new EU member states would gradually become more and more like them. Since trade, markets and democracy were considered to be inseparable, these were destined to strengthen each other ever more intimately over time. In the same vein, trade was expected to gradually and indirectly westernize China and Russia, through the WTO and the EU, respectively: *Wandel durch Handel* or 'Change through Trade', in the motto of the German Russia strategy. That view did not age well and is all set to change when the EU gets a geostrategic *raison d'être* that is aligned with a newly hardened world.

Common values, always more of an aspiration than a reality in international relations, no longer drive the international order. The supposed link between more economic freedom and prosperity, more political freedom and more individualism has failed in practice.[7] The receding tide of Communism revealed not an empty green field for universal liberalism but a reactionary brown field full of unprocessed history, civilizational revenge, religious traditions and identity politics. On that toxic breeding ground nationalism, populism and authoritarianism are growing globally, spilling over into a new battle of the great powers and a new war of civilization in Ukraine.[8] Even within the EU, culture and values have become a source of conflict and division, both within and between member states, especially for former Eastern Bloc countries with Slavic-Orthodox roots.

History has returned and the dreams have ended.[9] Raw domination, unapologetic power and cold realpolitik are back, having never quite left, not only in authoritarian regimes like China or Russia. The USA has traditionally stood for a foreign policy that combines American power with American idealism and messianism as a fountain of liberty in the world. But under US President Biden, Donald Trump's cry of 'America First' has become a mature doctrine in which economic and (geo)political cooperation serve a new global American leadership.[10] In that worldview, allies are not necessarily partners and partners are not necessarily allies. Into this fits, for example, a pivotal country like India, admittedly a crucial democracy we count on in the emerging new world order, but above all a country that since its independence has stood for unfettered autonomy and the primacy of national interests over values.[11] A values-driven international order, until recently idealized by the USA as a universal mission and symbolized by the EU in Europe, nowadays finds bitterly few adherents outside Europe that matter. Even President Biden's lofty 'Summit for Democracy', a new global initiative triggered by his belief that the twenty-first century will be defined by the competition between democracy and autocracy, includes not a few rather unfree countries, reflecting a pragmatic desire to unite as many countries as possible in a freedom dynamic while the world mostly suffers from a well-documented 'democratic recession'.[12]

In any case, gone is the globalization that stood for economic openness and cooperation and that was rooted in the underlying Washington Consensus to gradually bind the world more intimately together on the basis of trade, markets, rules and rights. Instead of inclusion, exclusion dominates. Instead of the world, blocs matter. America, China, Europe and other countries or regions with international heft now want autonomy and security first and foremost. Free trade represents interdependence. That was a strength in a world with a shared framework of values and norms, but it becomes a weakness when that framework disappears. For example, Russian gas and Chinese technology are then viewed not as cheap imports but as dangerous risks. We now want the trade that fits into a closed loop that supports our own strategic autonomy and national security. Meanwhile, a new consensus prevails in Washington that on balance and in practice amounts to degrees of economic nationalism.[13]

Globalization is not by definition incompatible with national interests such as strategic autonomy and security. One can bet on globalization to deliver reliable apolitical star companies and to deny politicized star companies to geopolitical competitors. A global market generates superstar firms of global scale that serve everyone for a profit while diminishing the importance of national corporate champions: just look at the mostly American global technology giants. But once the logic of de-globalization kicks in, it becomes self-fulfilling. If China under President Xi wants to lead the world with new Chinese industrial champions and dismisses the USA as a power in decline, the USA will eventually want to sell, lend and invest less in China, which will eventually make China want to become even more economically independent. At the same time, mutual trust is melting and distrust of trade relations is growing as geopolitical risk is forcing politics to increasingly supplant commerce. We have now truly entered that spiral of reciprocal and self-reinforcing de-globalization. Whether in technology, energy or commodities, international production chains, investment and capital flows will increasingly reflect the underlying geopolitical and political strategy, and decreasingly reflect the free allocation of investment and resources by companies and markets.

This trend is deepened further because governments have put themselves back behind the steering wheel of the economy. Whether their aim is to save the climate or biodiversity, to dominate the critical technology chains, to generate national business champions or to grow a middle class of new industrial jobs, countries everywhere are politicizing economic development and actively steering their economies towards public goals, a development we highlight in chapter 4 as being critical for the new EU.[14] The space for globalization is shrinking directly through geopolitics and indirectly through politicization, with a common denominator of economic nationalism and protectionism reinforcing each other.

Instead of the world being made ever flatter and more deeply connected through an increasingly level commercial and financial playing field,[15] the world is being divided and driven apart by nationalism and power blocs. International trade and investment are subordinated to national industrial policy and to international politics that beats to the rhythm of superpower and regional competition. Swapping geopolitical consensus for rivalry and conflict came first; swapping free trade for decoupling, de-risking, near-shoring, friend-shoring or national sovereignty – all variations of de-globalization practised around the world – followed.[16] Both feed into and reinforce each other. For all countries and regional blocs, the end of globalization means the need for a national or regional vision linking the economy, autonomy and security. Increasingly, trade and investment are becoming neither free nor open but conditional on and used for avoiding national or regional risk and building national or regional strength. Between market and power, technology and weapons, energy and security, money and violence, there is no longer any strategic distinction.

Economy = Geopolitics

This new global reality has stark implications for the EU as the former poster child of the bygone globalization era. The European Commission – the body where policy preparation, policy initiative and policy implementation come together in the EU – has consciously morphed from a technocratic bureaucracy for market forces and free trade agreements into an overtly 'geopolitical Commission'.[17] That tilt reflects how the EU must respond to the new world and how it must overcome its strategic vulnerability in the changed global context. But it is also a tilt with little backbone, as yet. It mainly underlines how economics, trade, investment and technology – collectively, the natural purview of the EU and its Commission – have become de facto geopolitics. It manifests a corresponding European strategic aspiration and purpose, not an institutionally strengthened EU adorned by member states with the trappings and tools for geopolitics – think, for instance, competences in foreign policy, cyber security or defence. The EU conducts geopolitics with the configuration of a free trade club. Mainly, this means repurposing trade and markets for other needs, on an ad hoc basis.

The first observation is that the EU's 'soft power' has become hard power in line with its changing circumstances. By standing still in a changed world, the economic EU has become a geopolitical union by default. The war in Ukraine has taught us that we can mobilize and play off the 'soft power' of that big European market for war purposes. We have declared war on Russia both economically and financially; although we are not on the battlefield, we are boycotting and squeezing the Russian war machine and energy industry. The EU has orchestrated a riot of sanctions that are cutting off the Russian economy, affecting its financial, technological and industrial sectors, its defence contractors, as well as the elite of the Putin regime.[18] Trade, finance and cyber technology are the weapons in a modern-day all-out war. Financial and trade sanctions are the equivalent of the intercontinental precision weapons that Europe, like imperial America before it, now unabashedly deploys extraterritorially against hostile countries, against suspicious international companies and against business moguls collaborating with the enemy.

Like the USA, the EU has recuperated and retooled the ties of globalization – a construct of a past geopolitical consensus – for geopolitical conflict and rivalry. The EU stands strong in weaponizing globalization thanks to its pivotal role in the European and the global economy. Europe is itself accelerating the end of globalization: if trade is a weapon, nobody wants trade relations except with privileged geopolitical partners. If everything becomes a potential weapon, then economics is potentially warfare and everyone is potentially a victim.[19]

At the same time, on Ukraine's battlefield, we see how commercial technology – mobile communications, 'do-it-yourself' drones, Starlink's satellites and so on – is inseparable from military technology, how software and artificial intelligence (AI) are the new tanks, and how civilian technology is being used and abused by enemies and allies alike for hybrid warfare on and off the battlefield. European economic integration is military integration when trade, money, energy and technology are weapons in cold, lukewarm or hot hybrid war realities. Whether we like it or not, the unified European market turns Europe into a new geopolitical power player, and the new geopolitics turns economics into power politics. Commercial relations, civilian technology or defence development: the distinction is blurring. Since it is blurring, the EU – the guardian of all things commercial and technological in Europe – cannot but play the power game with both feet.

The EU is naturally becoming a geopolitical power union as it fulfils its long-standing economic role in this new hostile world where economics is an extension of hard power and hard power an extension of economics. This evolution is happening at breakneck speed and the examples are legion:

- 2019: The EU coordinates the screening of foreign investments into Europe for strategic and security risks, ensuring that EU member states detect and block geopolitically undesirable investments. All European countries are expected to engage in geopolitical protectionism under a European umbrella, safeguarding their economies from suspicious foreign players.[20] The days of the likes of TikTok and Huawei in Europe are numbered, even if Europe lacks a centrally controlled list of foreign companies that are labelled suspicious or non grata, for now. The counterpart of organized restriction of European investments into high-risk countries, sectors and companies outside Europe also seems only a matter of time.
- 2021: The EU establishes the European Defence Fund (EDF) and the European Peace Facility (EPF). The EDF aims to contribute to European defence and security cooperation and coordination through research and development.[21] The EPF aims to contribute to conflict prevention, peace and security outside Europe.[22] Both funds remain relatively

limited in their financial clout: some €8 billion each until 2027. But their political relevance is great; they show how the EU is focusing its current budget on a distinct geopolitical and military mission both inside and outside Europe. In the absence of any new formal EU competence for defence, conflict and security, the EU is becoming a de facto conduit for European federalization in the fields of defence planning, military development and international conflict management. By 2023, allocated budgets have already been increased to €12 billion, which includes any additional support being provided to the Ukrainian army.[23]

- 2021: The EU initiates a regime for controlling export, trade and transit of items that may have dual civilian and military uses, including software and technology as well as items for the design, development, production and use of nuclear, chemical or biological weapons.[24] With the European Commission as a central hub, the EU thereby organizes a framework for monitoring and containing European exports and trade that may present geopolitical risks.

- 2021: The EU and the USA establish a joint Trade and Technology Council (TTC),[25] which is a forum through which to coordinate EU–US approaches to key global trade, economic and technology issues and to deepen transatlantic trade and economic relations. Through the TTC, the European Commission and the US federal government combine to geopolitically steer trade and technology.

- 2021: The EU develops a tool to counter the kind of economic coercion that third countries can exert on European countries and companies.[26] The Anti-Coercion Instrument (ACI) aims to prevent a superpower like China from restricting, or threatening to restrict, trade or investment in order to force policy changes in Europe. While the EU itself does not shy away from using economics as a weapon against hostile regimes, it has made sure to arm itself to respond to economic intimidation by hostile countries.

- 2021: The EU coordinates a European approach to defining and building European autonomy in critical economic and technological sectors.[27] The aim is to avoid European dependence in sectors that count as strategically important, including raw materials, pharmaceutical ingredients, batteries, hydrogen, semiconductors and cloud computing. The EU thus coordinates and facilitates its member states in building industrial and technological capacities to collectively ensure strategic European autonomy in geopolitical terms.

- 2021: The EU unveils the Global Gateway initiative, mobilizing €300 billion to invest in the infrastructure of developing countries outside Europe.[28] This is not European humanitarian largesse; rather, it is European geopolitics. Europe is aiming to counterbalance China, which, particularly through its Belt and Road Initiative or so-called New Silk Road, is fostering obedience in dozens of countries by funding or developing large-scale infrastructure projects with Chinese money or Chinese state-owned enterprises. China is also using Chinese state institutions such as the China Development Bank to finance strategic investments abroad. Adopting a similar approach in response, as of 2022 the EU tasks the European Investment Bank (EIB) – previously mainly an intra-European development bank – with a global investment mandate.[29]

- 2022: The EU is given the power to act against foreign subsidies that distort the European market.[30] This enables Europe to take controlling and remedial action when subsidy policies by countries outside Europe affect the economy in Europe, particularly through unfair competition by favoured companies. For example, without completely excluding a country like China from the European market, the EU will be able to intervene in a targeted way towards any Chinese companies that threaten to corner the European market thanks to Chinese state aid. Gone are the days when countries and companies could take advantage of Europe's patience under globalization to steal market share with unfair trade practices, safe in the knowledge that the WTO would take many years to judge any complaint on technical merits. In the new geopolitics of trade, the EU is simply able to respond unilaterally to defend its home market.

- 2022: Through the European Chips Act, the EU aims to address semiconductor shortages in Europe, facilitate large-scale investments and strengthen Europe's technological leadership.[31] Semiconductors are a sector in which the EU wants to avoid becoming dependent on non-European countries that pose geopolitical risks to Europe.

- 2022: Through the European Medicines Agency, the EU establishes its power to manage the flow of medicines and medical devices across Europe in the event of a European public health crisis.[32] The Covid-19 pandemic demonstrates the geopolitical importance of producing and distributing medicines and medical devices across national borders. Building on this, the EU lays the foundation of a veritable Health Union that develops European control over the strategic chain of production and supply in case of emergencies.

- 2023: Through legislation in support of ammunition production, the EU contributes to the responsiveness and capability of the European defence industry and to the rapid delivery of ammunition and missiles in Europe.[33] In the context of the war in Ukraine, this is the first step towards coordinating industrial ammunition and weapons production in the EU.

- 2023: The EU develops a robust emergency tool to keep the European single market crisis-proof.[34] This includes building up European reserves of goods and services that are deemed strategically important, monitoring supply chains and directing production in case of crisis – all under EU control and with enforced cooperation from countries and companies alike. With this mechanism, the EU, following the USA's example, is taking an important step towards coordinating strategic European economic capacity for geopolitical agility in case of emergencies.

The EU's starting position as the guardian of the European single market thus spontaneously put it in pole position for European superpower politics. From that pole position, we see, right before our eyes, how the new geopolitical needs are propelling a proto-federal EU at a speed and with a scope that is truly breathtaking when measured against the complexity of the EU's decision-making processes. Of course, decision-making and implementation can be two different things, for the EU as for any government. Moreover, the EU is not necessarily endowed with the instruments or the budgets to force EU-wide action and compliance, implying risks of delay or overload in some of its flagship initiatives. However, the new wave of EU superpower policies is typically more centralizing than before, positioning the EU as the main actor and reducing reliance on collective member state action. In this, too, the EU is taking strides towards becoming a veritable power union.

Power Union

Internally federalizing the EU into a fledgling power union is the EU member states' common response to an external world that is demanding that Europe be a power bloc. Without the EU power union, European countries would have to suffer as the world tilts from a Europe-friendly unipolar order to either a new cold war of bipolar competition between the USA and China or a chaotic and risky multipolar global disorder. Without the EU power union, the hostile world would act as a centrifugal force, tearing apart the cohesion among the European countries and causing them to scramble for national interests. Europe's values and its interests require a strong EU that can be both a partner to the USA and a bridge to the rest of the world.

That economics is becoming unadulterated power as the dial turns from globalization to global conflict and de-globalization, and that the EU is subjecting the European economy to geo-politics in a quasi-federal fashion, also go a long way towards explaining why, in economic matters in general, the EU is trad-ing the market for the state. But more on that later. First, I want to stress what the EU must achieve in order to be and remain itself in this new global power reality: a strong, internationally focused and therefore necessarily European military capabil-ity. I do this not out of any antagonism towards allies, the USA first and foremost. Indeed, I believe that the transatlantic alliance, with its military crowning achievement in NATO, is itself entering a phase of broadening and deepening not unlike that of the EU, precisely because military logic is seeping into the civil domain: in trade, in technology, in digitalization and so on.

But I embrace the same conviction that the USA embraces in NATO: almost eighty years after the end of the Second World War, we in Europe have to pay our own bills. We can no longer outsource our collective security to the USA, with or without Donald Trump in the White House. We can no longer 'free ride' on the Pax Americana, even if we wanted to. Nor can we expect that NATO will always be ready in the future to solve Europe's security challenges. The USA has its hands full all over the world. Unless NATO transforms into a global alli-ance, Europe must acquire autonomous military force that is in parallel with and complementary to NATO. And paying for our own defence and military would mean that we also decide when and where to deploy it – which would forge a much deeper relationship with the USA than we can achieve in our present position of strategic and operational subordination.

Europe must be able to stand with America, together or separately, according to its interests. The reality that soft power has become hard power is having an equally transformative impact on the relationship between the EU and the USA. For one thing, the historic distinction between the economic EU and the military NATO is no longer valid. An EU that continues to neglect or delegate hard military power cannot carry out its economic, technology and energy missions with the necessary European autonomy. An EU that remains dependent on NATO is a union that remains partly indebted to the USA in relation to the geopolitics of economic growth, technology and energy. If Europe wants any agility in shaping the new international order, it must become stronger and more self-reliant as a military power, for me together with the USA where possible or necessary, and equally together with countries that want to continue to espouse the democratic and trade values of the previous period.

Europe's military self-reliance is necessary in a world where Europe is once again a geostrategic fault line, where America has to compete with China, and where the Free West in general is once more in rivalry and conflict with another civilizational model with global aspirations. China wants to become the centre of a new world order based on three 'global initiatives' – global development, global security and global civilization – all under Chinese control and greased with Chinese money, Chinese investment and access to the Chinese market.[35] With the large carrot of development aid, loans and investments, China is seducing countries into accepting alternative platforms for multilateral relations, thereby gaining supporters to mobilize for a Chinese agenda in traditional international institutions such as the UN.[36]

The EU cannot afford internal geopolitical divisions in relation to China and must be able to offer a unified alternative and counterweight to China vis-à-vis third countries. 'Speaking softly while carrying a big stick' is also the way to deal constructively and convincingly with the many non-aligned countries, if only to shore up their security when they do align with us. Hard military power is the continuation of moral and economic influence by other means, and vice versa. If we do not want to squander the legacy of the previous generations that steered us out of the Cold War and into globalization, we must combine and integrate soft power with hard power. The two cannot survive separately.

Building on the recent example of the aforementioned EDF, the EU must gradually coordinate and streamline more of a European defence capability, gradually enabling NATO to become a US–European duopoly. Without technological capability there is no defence capability; hence, the EU will also need to link commercial technology to defence and security. It can achieve this partly through building autonomous European capability in chips, AI and satellites, for example; partly through coordinating with the USA by way of the joint TTC, for example; and partly by decoupling from Chinese suppliers such as Huawei. And the EU has already acquired all of the tools necessary for this, as we have seen.

Currently the EU is working on a framework for a Common Security and Defence Policy that is focused on international peacekeeping and conflict prevention.[37] The framework is only in the embryonic stage, but if the EU can grow it into a truly European foreign policy strategy, it will achieve a dream that used to be purely a French dream: no defence Europe is conceivable without a geopolitical Europe, just as no full-fledged geopolitical Europe is conceivable without a defence Europe. If the EU is to stand up to defend its international interests alongside the USA and NATO, it must first be able to determine what the common European interests are.

Of course, all this is much easier said than done. The reality is still that European countries, especially the large EU member states, collectively do not trust each other enough and individually trust themselves too much to achieve European strategic synergy. The geopolitical EU outlined here is real and moving fast, but it is driven by the EU's previously acquired position in economics and trade, and by the urgencies of war and crisis. Thus, it incrementally layers geopolitics onto the institutional architecture of an EU that remains primarily a trade and market union; it is not the emanation of a renewed EU with a geopolitical finality and a mature federal architecture to match. In areas such as cyber security, counter-intelligence, foreign policy, development cooperation and investment policy outside Europe, there is much less spontaneous European convergence and coordination. In defence, the collective comfort of NATO continues to anaesthetize, divide and suppress the EU. If the EU does not grow into a full-fledged power union, it risks ending up as an extension of US geopolitics, except this time without the strategic weight that Europe had as the international front line during the first Cold War.[38]

The opportunity and the momentum are there. The new need for geopolitics and hard power applies to everyone: to individual EU member states separately and to the EU as a whole. Everyone in Europe recognizes the need for more geopolitics in Europe. The only question is how: through Brussels or through Paris and Berlin? The sheer number and complexity of the countries involved mean that such evolution cannot happen without the EU itself being involved. If the countries of the EU want to weigh in on geopolitics individually, they must do it at least partly collectively through the EU. If the EU wants to remain relevant in this new era in world history, it must become at least partly the forum of European power politics. If we all need to rediscover the importance of hard power, both nationally and Europe-wide, why not scale it up to be Europe-wide right away?

Take Germany, to name the elephant in the Western European room. After two world wars, the EU and NATO together settled the historic German question – 'too big for Europe, too small for the world' – with pacification and integration. But the German question is now back in a new form. Germany can no longer count on Russia for cheap energy, or on China for cheap manufacturing and exports, or on the USA for security. Either we can address this new German question under the umbrella of the EU, or we risk seismic shifts within the EU as Germany and other major countries reinvent themselves geopolitically.

To name just one example, it is of course right and necessary for a country like Germany to devise a formal China strategy for the very first time, reflecting the rebirth of geopolitics in Europe and sensibly hinting at scaling down German presence and investment in China.[39] After all, German industry is dangerously dependent on China as both an outlet and a supplier and the Chinese regime is only too happy to keep German multinationals addicted to the Chinese market, to co-opt them as a pressure group in the geopolitical dynamics between China and Europe. But it is just as necessary and even better for the German China strategy to subscribe to a European China strategy, which the European Commission itself promotes under the term 'de-risking'.[40] In fact, the two are happening simultaneously: the German China strategy explicitly wants to support a European China strategy that is not conceivable without German consent. Both strategies cannot but integrate if they are to be successful. Reluctantly, organically, the drive towards a geopolitical EU is thus coming to life.

And China is just the symbolic tip of the iceberg. With the end of globalization, trade relations by definition have become geopolitical relations. Trade is now conditional on and expressive of underlying geopolitical relationships in the new world order. The EU has the exclusive power to negotiate international trade agreements in Europe and to impose international trade sanctions from Europe. Inevitably, then, it must pursue a strategy of international politics. Synergy in foreign policy between the EU and its member states is crucial. There is of course some space between economic and political relations, between the extent to which a third country can conduct free trade with the EU and develop political relations with individual EU member states. While that space can hold a degree of tension, it can hardly accommodate a contradiction between EU policy and member state policy. With third countries that really matter geopolitically, aligning foreign policy within Europe and through the EU becomes plainly necessary, reducing the scope for any national 'special relationships'. Hence the example of the German China strategy. And hence the EU controlling the sanctions regime against Russia while enveloping the real national political differences with regard to Russia in a European compromise at every turn.

At a later stage, the EU as a mature power union will increasingly be able to hold strategic control and determine the overall direction of foreign policy, thereby also forging a growing intimacy between geopolitics and defence in Europe. The logic for this is equally technological and industrial. We will see in chapter 4 how the EU aims to make the economy across Europe more sustainable, more autonomous and more resilient through climate and industrial policies. Realizing the European strategies for both climate and industry crucially depends on having a robust European geopolitical strategy, given the state of flux in the world order. New supply chains and transport infrastructure for importing both renewable and fossil energy into Europe, supplying the raw materials and components for a battery economy in Europe, ensuring access to the building blocks of an autonomous European chips industry: all this is necessary and it is all to be negotiated with countries we seek to reliably place in our geopolitical camp.[41]

It is no coincidence that top EU representatives have been working overtime through an inflation of diplomatic missions to Africa, the Middle East and Asia, in search of partners and partnerships for energy, raw materials and technology. Over a period of just a few years, the EU has concluded agreements with China, India, Japan, Israel, Morocco, Tunisia, Egypt, South Korea, Saudi Arabia, Vietnam, Qatar, the United Arab

Emirates, Mongolia, Indonesia, Algeria, Nigeria, Thailand, South Africa and Bahrain, in addition to more general renewable energy initiatives with the Gulf region, Africa and Asia.[42] This is hyperactive superpower Europe in full swing driving the symbiosis of European trade policy and European foreign policy against the backdrop of a new geopolitical reality in which both allied and competing countries are striving for the same goals, with the EU as the political spearhead both inside and outside Europe.

Border Union

Power and security also mean borders. The EU – itself a territorial expression of geostrategy – is also, as a matter of course, a border union. This is an inconvenient truth for the European project, which has long been built on dismantling borders. Here again, defence, civilian, economic and geostrategic matters merge in and through the EU. In defence matters, EU member states are major partners in an enlarged NATO with new external borders; just look at the recent accession to NATO of EU member states Finland and Sweden. In civil matters, the EU is responsible for guaranteeing a basic rule-of-law migration order and basic human rights on European territory – up to now a real stain on the European record – as well as for public health through a post-Covid-19 Health Union that includes a coordinated border policy. In economic matters, the EU is developing and safeguarding economic strength that excludes extraterritorial dependence on geopolitical adversaries. In geostrategic matters, the EU is cultivating mature relationships with the countries at the limits of its territory and sphere of influence. Mature means something other than paying for subcontracting that leads to subordination and dependence of the EU in controlling refugee flows, to cite just the infamous example of the EU–Turkey refugee deal.

Since the civil war in Syria, Europe has been the scene of a refugee crisis. Here, too, crisis has paved the way for European power politics. As part of its expansion towards Central Europe, the EU established Frontex in 2004 as an agency to coordinate operations at its external borders. In response to the sudden refugee crisis in 2015, Frontex was immediately rigged for genuine border and coastguard surveillance, including maritime security, security checks, and search and rescue operations. Frontex is now on track to increase its staff numbers and annual budget tenfold by 2025, complemented by a unified standing corps of 10,000 active border guards assembled by member states.[43] The EU may not have a formal army, but its borders are guarded by a de facto European army commanded by a European agency. On the ground, Frontex has single-handedly introduced a new European culture and practice of tough border control.[44] I am not commenting here on its legitimacy, expediency or effectiveness, but I will say that it would be hard to get much closer to a federal European power union. Power is sometimes dirty and sometimes painful to watch, but the EU no longer has the luxury of keeping its hands clean while other countries do the dirty work. The alternative – refugee chaos and growing tensions among EU member states – would be worse.

Europe's unprecedented structural refugee crisis and the explosive demographic realities at its external borders may even bridge the bitter divides over national migration policies in Europe. The biggest supporters of 'Fortress Europe' are now the most generous hosts of Ukrainian war refugees. We can build on this: with European solidarity, support and distribution to relieve countries like Poland and Hungary, but also Southern Europe; and with a mature European policy that combines security, border control, law and order, economic migration and refugee policy. For this, in our geographically vulnerable and demographically ageing continent, there are both humanitarian and economic needs, and now also pressing strategic ones.

The historic migration agreement of December 2023 is a symbolic step in that direction. It marks the beginning of a federalized European immigration zone connected to unified European external borders. It is based on internal European openness (where countries must serve as hosts for asylum seekers, regardless of state borders) and solidarity (where countries must either receive refugees or contribute financially) – which nods to the strength of the old values-driven EU – but also on stricter border enforcement and the disciplining of neighbouring countries to prevent irregular arrivals and increase returns: the omens of a new power union that also weighs extraterritorially.[45] This pragmatic agreement is not an end point but a tentative starting point. Differences and divisions remain. The tension between values and interests remains acute, such as in using Tunisia as a buffer state against uncontrolled migration to Europe. But it is a remarkable precedent in the EU's transformation towards a power union. While migration and asylum remain in a state of crisis, the new EU has achieved a legal framework that surpasses that of the USA in organizing collaboration and solidarity between frontline and inland states. It now must ensure its proper implementation on the ground.

The new power union will indeed require more European strategic autonomy and operational capacity because the EU must be able to dominate or at least influence its geography: the Balkans, the Mediterranean region including Turkey and North Africa, the de facto buffer states vis-à-vis Russia on the Baltic Sea and in Eastern Europe, regardless of Ukraine's eventual status. In achieving this, the EU must be able to counter the interference of strategic adversaries, Russia and China foremost among them. It must be able to maintain unified borders. It must be able to enforce European territorial interests without being dependent on NATO support – just think

of Turkey's veto position in NATO. It must be able to provide security and protection support to peripheral countries
it wishes to include in its geostrategic orbit, again regardless
of whether these countries are formal members of the EU. In
essence, the EU must become for its periphery what the USA
was for Western Europe during the Cold War, either alone or
in close cooperation with the same USA.

Peace requires power, we realize once again. A geostrategic
Europe cannot exist without a European defence capability
that is at the level of our prosperity, our European strategic
needs and our global aspirations. European defence has been
talked about for a long time. Until there is a European military
strategy, an infrastructure and a command structure, however,
this is just talk. Are we prepared for an appointed European
leadership, over and against the wishes of this or that member
state, to put European men and women in the line of fire? Until
we are, defence autonomy is wishful thinking, however desirable and indispensable it may seem.

Transforming the EU into a bulwark of hard European
power in a hardened world will happen by fits and starts
because it requires new coordination between countries and/
or new EU powers. Sooner or later, EU member states will have
to get back to answering the real questions of power that we
have neglected or left to the Americans for many decades.

We need to guard our external borders in the face of a
demographic and refugee reality that our welfare states cannot
cope with. We need to rearm. We must reduce strategic
dependence on countries that do not share our position on
the value scale or in the world order. We need to mobilize civil
communication technology, computer technology and space
technology – and the value chains behind them – as weapons.
Because of the changed world, the formerly economic EU has
automatically become a military and security project. It will be
up to us, the democratic nation-states on the European continent, to draw the consequences from this for the next phase of

European cooperation and integration, in our well-understood common self-interest.

In any case, where no new EU powers are needed or where member states withhold from transferring more powers from their national sovereignty to a renewed EU, the spontaneous transformation of the EU into a power union is already a reality. Old powers are being reinvented for a new age. Which brings me to the biggest change in the day-to-day reality of the EU: the pendulum swing from the market to the state.

4

A State Project

A Proto-federal EU State

The transformation of the EU into both a geostrategic coalition and a power union has a common denominator in that geography, borders and geopolitics are the natural terrain and the core mission of the sovereign nation-state. If we elevate these in Europe to the level of the EU, then the EU instantly and obviously becomes a quasi-federal European superstate as a matter of fact.

Take the overview of new EU policy at the intersection of economics and geopolitics as discussed in the previous chapter, and compare it with what is happening in the USA. Screening foreign investment for strategic and security risks, funding defence research and planning, organizing international conflict prevention, restricting commercial exports that present military or security risks, countering third countries exercising economic coercion or unfair competition, building strategic capacity in critical economic and technological sectors, funding strategic investment abroad, organizing strategic autonomy in chips, coordinating and funding ammunition production, coordinating the production and distribution of medicines and medical devices in the event of a public health crisis, crisis-proofing the economy in the event of an emergency: the USA is also doing or developing all that. It is initiated or coordinated there at the federal level, by presidential decree, by the federal government and/or by federal agencies, sometimes coordinated through federal legislation or overseen by committees in the federal Congress.[1]

Under President Biden, the USA is also leaving globalization and subjecting the US economy and trade to geostrategy and geopolitics, with a focus on American reindustrialization, technological leadership and strategic autonomy.[2] Much of what the EU is doing in this regard, moreover, is inspired by, in cooperation with or in response to the USA. But here is the catch: the USA is a constitutional federal state. President Biden was elected with a mandate to ready America for an era of new geopolitical rivalry with China. President Biden is the constitutional commander-in-chief, working with the constitutionally federalized departments of defence and national security to respond to the war in Ukraine with American policy.

The EU lacks a mature and transparent democratic federal architecture. The transformation of the EU towards big-state EU federalism is mainly the fruit of *mission creep*, of successive waves of crisis policies under great pressure, of incremental Europeanization without an overarching agenda, decided at conclaves of heads of government and prepared by diplomacy and bureaucracy. This is de facto European federalization according to the wisdom of founding father Jean Monnet: through the polycrisis of our time, through reaction to events (think Harold Macmillan's 'events, dear boy').

When crisis strikes, it is usually 'the state first and last': the government takes charge as the ultimate guardian and all politics becomes spontaneously national. Just think of the bank and other corporate bailouts during the banking crisis and the subsequent Great Recession (2008–9), of state borders during a refugee crisis (2015), of national security during the pandemic

(2020–2). In Europe, however, it is not the nation-state but the EU that has been the big-state winner in the major crises of our time. The EU has managed to transcend national interests by providing what the European nation-states either could not provide for themselves – or could not do alone without threatening the EU itself: free money to safeguard the eurozone, vaccines for public health, post-pandemic recovery funds, an energy cartel for maximum prices during the Ukraine war, a war reset for economic relations with Russia, and a multinational response to global warming that inherently transcends all national boundaries.

When there is a crisis in Europe, the EU is always part of the answer. As a result, the EU has continued to evolve as an autonomous state actor, as a proto-federal state entity that organically and in times of crisis sucks up national sovereignty and comes ever closer to the fait accompli of an EU state. The division of roles between member states and the EU is blurring and tilting towards European federalization, without the constitutional set-up of the EU itself having evolved along with it from bureaucratic or institutional to democratic federal decision-making.

The quasi-revolutionary decisiveness of the EU at our juncture contrasts sharply with the incapacity of national democracies. Across Europe, societies are polarizing; populism and culture wars are raging; party politics is fragmenting into a mosaic of ever more and ever smaller political parties; and voters are changing affiliations and majorities as if they were shirts.[3] The impotence of democratic national politics paradoxically is giving a considerable amount of space and power to the technocratic politics of the EU.

Quirks of personalities and politics aside, it is not surprising that this new phase of European integration is being led by an emboldened European Commission and its bureaucracy, supported benevolently by the major member states, rather than by the collegial forum of national government leaders that is the European Council of member states. When the EU needs the decisiveness, speed and dirigisme of a de facto state, there is no escaping its uniquely proto-federal administration that is the European Commission.

Quantitatively, the EU has become larger and more complex: it has more member states with more diversity. Qualitatively, the national democracies of its member states are struggling with political fragmentation and polarization. It is increasingly difficult to build upon the complexity of national political coalitions the European coalitions that generate sufficient democratic representativeness at EU level. The EU's transformation is the triumph of European technocracy and bureaucracy, under the leadership of pragmatic national heads of government at decisive moments of European summits. The familiar 'democratic deficit' of a supranational EU – the perennial observation that much of what the EU decides owes little to direct democratic decisions and legitimacy – is inevitably larger and more acute than ever before.

The sudden and de facto partial federalization of the EU is much more than the sum of pragmatic crisis responses to external events, however. It hides a fundamental turning point. The paradigm shift towards the state in the EU goes far beyond the intersection between economics and power under the pressure of world disorder. The primacy of geostrategy and geopolitics in the EU implies the primacy of politics over the market in Europe. A geopolitical EU must be able to dictate, mould, mobilize and/or shield the European economy for geopolitical purposes, both offensively and defensively. Transforming the EU thus goes deeper and further than meets the eye. It touches on the essential identity of the EU itself: the EU began life as a bastion of the free market but is becoming a bastion of statism and politicization over markets.

Statism versus Markets

After the end of the Second World War, the European integration that would lead to the EU began as centralized European
control over the war industry. European pooling and steering
of industrial capacity in coal and steel, and atomic energy –
indirectly preventing those materials from being mobilized by
any one nation for its own war planning – was the *raison d'être*
of the European Coal and Steel Community (ECSC) and the
European Atomic Energy Community (Euratom), respectively:
it fostered a wartime-oriented security community.

In this sense, then, the EU began as a controlling state project. It gradually became dominantly an innovative market
project: the European single market – which was inscribed
as a mere objective in the original basic European treaty –
was politically and legally realized just over thirty years ago,
in 1993. The heart of the EU, the foundation of the forward-
looking European integration project, thus became a European
economic community, a unified free internal market, in due
course crowned by a currency union.[4]

The European Economic Community that would in time
come to form the core of the EU became an open single market
based on economic and personal freedoms and underpinned
by a separation of governments and the economy, coupled
with an external common European policy of treaty-based free
trade. Both internally and externally, therefore, the EU came
to stand for a free market where state ownership, control,
regulation, intervention and support were either gradually
dismantled or carefully scrutinized as potentially problematic
and market distorting, all of it steered and supervised by the
independent bureaucracy of the European Commission.[5]

The currency union meant the common euro, a common
monetary policy and a European Central Bank (ECB) with a
'Bundesbank bis' narrow mandate focused on price stability;
it effectively severed currency and interest rate policies from

political manipulation. However, the eurozone as it stands lacks the institutional foundations of a normal currency union, notably a banking union and a fiscal union with the capacity to tax, spend and redistribute both to steer the economy and to facilitate economic convergence among its member states. Instead, eurozone member states individually sign up to the collective Stability and Growth Pact: a common commitment to limit overall budget deficits and levels of public debt. This is again overseen by the European Commission through what is known as the European Semester: a framework for governing and managing the fiscal policies of every member state within common boundaries of frugality that is sometimes decried as austerity by its opponents.[6]

A market with little government interference, with a currency independent from politics, and with little government debt: that was the essence of the EU as a supranational project that otherwise left wide discretion to national member states and their domestic powers. It was an excellent fit: modest governments mean no unfair competition through government interference, no crowding out of smaller or poorer member states by larger or richer ones. A stable open market and currency union mean a macroeconomic 'level playing field': the same fair opportunities for all, regardless of differences in wealth and economic development. The EU was a perfect fit for an open world of trade and cooperation. There was always slack, but the large unified single market was the value proposition that linked the diversity of countries with diverse national interests in a European project that benefited everyone. Despite the inevitable ripples and controversies, the European common market impressively kept its promise of overall shared progress across business and enlargement cycles.[7]

However, open markets are often luxury goods: they are conceivable only if the security and the minimum shared values among the participating countries are such as to limit competition between the national interests to degrees of shared prosperity and growth. That was the essence of the EU itself and of the wider globalization for which it was a model – and it has since changed completely, as we have seen. The key question is: to what extent does the EU transforming into a geostrategic power project mean the end of the EU as a free-market haven, both within Europe and vis-à-vis third countries?

The changing world order is not the only force bending the strategic finality of the EU and forcing a new balance between governments and markets in Europe. There is also climate and environmental change. Here, an ambitious EU has opted for a dramatically different paradigm: 'Becoming the world's first climate-neutral continent by 2050' is now the official and dominant European mantra. The EU has hoisted itself upon the throne to decree and organize a transversal post-carbon transformation of societies and economies throughout Europe.[8] The EU that makes the market, guards it from government interference and unleashes it for open competition, innovation, growth and trade is now transforming itself through the 'NextGen EU' and the 'European Green Deal' into a protector and restorer of biodiversity, a climate planner, climate regulator, climate investor and climate tax authority.

The original EU wanted to maximize opportunities for growth and prosperity in Europe through a common European market. The new EU wants to subject the common European market to, or mobilize it for, climate, environment and biodiversity objectives. Sustainability, not growth, has become the primary economic focus of the EU. This implies state planning on a Chinese scale, in the Chinese style, partly transforming European institutions into biodiversity and climate institutions along the way. The EIB was primarily the bank for infrastructure and cohesion and is now also the European climate bank.[9] The ECB was the protector of price stability in the eurozone and is now also the driver of sustainable financing for the green transition.[10]

The European Commission, in particular, is undergoing a metamorphosis. Historically and by virtue of the EU's foundational treaty, the European Commission is the protector of the European free market. To this end, it is equipped with the full palette of state powers: regulation, supervision, policing, administering justice, execution and punishment. Like no other, the European Commission symbolizes an EU in which the member states unitedly separate the market from the state and jointly transfer the guarantees for this separation to the EU.[11] That same European Commission is now also and perhaps especially the coordinator that is trading market forces for strategic European or national statism, for example:

- 2019: Through the aforementioned 'European Green Deal', the European Commission becomes the central planner and coordinator of the path to climate neutrality across the European economy by 2050. The first stage is to achieve a 55 per cent emissions reduction by 2030. To this end, the Commission orchestrates and oversees the large-scale top-down greening of economic sectors in all EU member states, including funding with some €600 billion in subsidies by 2027.[12]
- 2020: Through its 'Biodiversity Strategy for 2030', the European Commission aims to plan and guide nature conservation, nature restoration and nature protection in Europe. Accordingly, the Commission sets a battery of both qualitative and quantitative targets that member states must achieve by 2030: for forests, marine areas, marine ecosystems, agricultural areas, pesticides, organic farming, rivers, trees, animal species, cities and so on.[13] Backed up by a comprehensive Nature Restoration Law,[14] EU member states are thus formally required to either link economic development to biodiversity or subordinate it to biodiversity targets.
- 2020: The European Commission begins organizing the transition to an economy that places less pressure on

natural resources through a 'Circular Economy Action Plan'. Consequently, the Commission imposes compulsory initiatives for, among others, sustainable products, circular electronics including a consumer right to repair, less plastic, reusable packaging, better textiles and less 'fast fashion'.[15] The EU's environmental strategy shifts from environmental standards to overall sustainability, which means that Europe is intervening more deeply in the structures and the business models of economic activity itself, forcing transformations to achieve politically determined sustainability goals.[16]

• 2020: Through its European industrial strategy, the European Commission plans and steers the transition not only to climate neutrality but also to digital leadership and the strategic autonomy of the European economy in the international context. This entails proactively providing political guidance and support, in cooperation with member states, sectors and companies, to favoured industrial ecosystems across the EU, including space and defence, agribusiness, construction, digital and electronics industries, energy-intensive industries, renewables, mobility and transport, automotives and textiles.[17]

• 2021: Through a programme for 'Important Projects of Common European Interest' (IPCEI), the European Commission is selecting and subsidizing bottom-up industrial projects that respond to top-down political priorities, in particular the implementation of the European Industrial Strategy, the European Data Strategy and the Green Deal. Approved projects cluster tens of billions of euros in funding from European and national state aid with co-investment from the private sector, including in energy, microelectronics, batteries and hydrogen.[18] In the same vein, the European Innovation Fund uses the many billions raised through the EU's emissions trading system to select and subsidize decarbonization projects for European industry on a grand scale.[19]

• 2023: Through its European Economic Security Strategy, the European Commission aims to coordinate public policies and public–private partnerships to avoid strategic risks in Europe. Priorities include strengthening the resilience of supply chains and energy security, safeguarding the physical and cyber security of critical infrastructure, as well as protecting technology security and preventing technology leakage, and countering the use of economic dependence or economic coercion as a weapon.[20] As a first step, the Commission has recommended a collective risk assessment across all member states for semiconductors, AI, quantum computing and biotechnology, the outcome of which will determine whether the EU will adopt a promote, protect or partner approach in any of these technology areas.[21] Further categories, including energy, robotics and manufacturing technology, could be added in the near future.

• 2023: Through a European strategy for autonomy in critical raw materials and the Critical Raw Materials Act (CRMA), the European Commission aims to organize reliable and sustainable supply chains for a wide range of specific sectors in Europe, including net-zero industry, digital industry, aerospace and defence. Among other things, the strategy establishes political quotas of minimum internal European capacity throughout the strategic supply chain by 2030, including for the extraction, processing and recycling of politically labelled 'critical raw materials', again the stepping stone to large-scale planning and subsidization.[22]

• 2023: Through the Net-Zero Industry Act (NZIA), the European Commission intends to install a preferential regime for technology projects that are politically chosen as being strategic for moving towards net-zero emissions, including a target of 40 per cent European autonomy. In particular, these projects relate to photovoltaic and solar thermal technologies, onshore and offshore renewable technologies, battery and storage technologies, heat pumps and geothermal energy technologies, electrolysis and fuel cells, biogas or biomethane technologies, and carbon capture and storage (CCS).[23]

The sum of all of this is clear. The EU that previously stood as a free trade zone exponent of globalization is being moulded into a body of de-globalization and top-down ecological, industrial and emissions planning, combined with an ever-expanding list of politically favoured technologies and sectors, all lubricated with lavish subsidy schemes.[24]

In trade policy, we no longer believe in strength through connectedness. These days, it is strength through autonomy that counts: connectedness is dangerous, after all. We are separating from Russia and diversifying away from China – no longer depending, but decoupling, de-risking, deterring, defending: it sounds like military terminology. We are following – albeit hesitantly – the US example in the pursuit of 'strategic autonomy' in an ever-lengthening list of industrial and technological sectors where it is not market and trade but instead government, industrial policy and government subsidies that set the tone.[25]

The EU that was modelled on German budgetary rigour is now the EU that trades budgetary discipline for debt politics. With 'cheap money' from an ECB that has become the permanent 'lender of last resort' in Europe since the euro crisis. With more than €700 billion of relief money via a European Recovery Fund – the historical precedent of European debt creation – after the pandemic.[26] With an EDF to develop pan-European military capabilities without European defence competence.[27] The EU, originally designed to discipline its member states fiscally, now funds and facilitates budget deficits in Europe. In addressing the pandemic, in the climate transition to net zero, in the new cold war with China and Russia, in the race for European economic sovereignty, everyone is letting public money roll and debts mount. The euro is no longer an instrument for fiscal discipline, serving instead as an instrument for debt politics: the strength and the flexibility of the euro enable more public debt than financial markets would otherwise tolerate from individual countries with national currencies. And, of course, sovereign debt means governments generating debt by becoming major economic actors.

The DNA of the old EU was to separate politics from economics. The DNA of the new EU is to mix politics and economics. The new EU tilts from market capitalism to state capitalism, focusing not on free-market forces but on state control and state intervention. This is the common denominator of European climate policy, biodiversity policy, industrial policy, geopolitical and monetary European policy, the war of sanctions against Russia and the new 'made in the EU' agenda for chips, solar panels, wind turbines, batteries and heat pumps, among other things. The EU that was the poster child of globalization has effectively done a U-turn to become a key player in de-globalization through a mix of state planning, subsidy races, strategic autonomy and state ownership policies, and through the geopolitical trade restrictions we have already listed.

Climate and war: behold the double magnet uniting the two sides of the political spectrum towards a state-centred EU, both at national and at European levels. Progressives and greens embrace climate and nature restoration policies while conservatives and economic liberals embrace industrial and security policies, both ending up in state activism, both overlapping in large-scale industrial planning and mega-subsidies. Much of this transformation is a pragmatic or logical adaptation to, or definition of, the changed strategic environment: it is the economic expression of the new strategic and ecological mission that the EU is undertaking with and for its member states. But it has consequences that eat away at the heart of the European project.

Politicization versus Markets

State intervention is contagious. Those who can dominate and direct the market in critical sectors, those who can subjugate the market to geopolitics or ecology, generally find regulating the market for political purposes to be self-evident. It is no coincidence that the EU's role transformation is coinciding with its own renewed regulatory drive. The EU that once stood for a free market is becoming an EU that makes the market more unfree. I give some notable recent examples:

- In everything digital, the European economy lags behind in innovation but leads the way in regulation: financial markets, the Internet, digital markets and soon AI. The main purpose of a regulated market is to serve fair competition, but onerous rules mean major obstacles for companies wanting to enter the market, which often has the effect of entrenching big businesses as market makers. For instance, Internet companies and big banks have to perform government tasks as 'gatekeepers' – especially focusing on privacy, data control, security and fraud prevention. Such regulatory burdens entrench corporate 'bigness' and forge a nexus between governments and corporations. The EU initially stood for making and guarding a European 'open market' in which national regulation for political goals had to be justified in principle as a potential obstacle to European trade.[28] It now stands for a priori European regulation to forge a 'fair market' that defines political objectives and sometimes delegates them to big business for 'market surveillance'.[29]
- In de-globalization for the sake of geopolitics, the EU is also organizing the politicization and bureaucratization of the European market. Screening exports and imports for strategic and security risks, anchoring capacity to strengthen European strategic autonomy, building European value chains in critical sectors, coordinating European arms

development and production: it all sounds logical and pure. But between European geopolitics, national protectionism and industrial favouritism, the boundaries are very murky. Geopolitics in theory means politics in practice. Restricting and steering the market geopolitically inevitably involves regulations and subsidies that disadvantage some market players while favouring others.

• In the pieces of globalization that remain, the EU is also in the business of recuperating commercial relationships for a purely political agenda. Major European companies will soon be required to impose European social and environmental standards on their foreign trading partners.[30] In the same vein, anyone seeking to import into Europe raw materials that are linked to deforestation and forest degradation in other parts of the world will have to prove sustainable origin.[31] This will mean strict standards and heavy bureaucracy outside Europe for producers and suppliers of beef, soy, palm oil, coffee, cocoa and rubber, among other things. Imports to Europe will soon be subject to import taxes – the so-called Carbon Border Adjustment Mechanism (CBAM) – if their production is too carbon-intensive by European emissions standards,[32] while the EU and the USA are building a cartel to protect 'sustainable' steel and aluminium from imports that were not produced with the same emissions standards.[33] In essence, the EU is forcing its switch towards climate and sustainability on trade relations outside Europe in an attempt to politically level the playing field for economic competition, thereby protecting both European companies and the planet.

• In the European labour market, a success story of the EU's eastward expansion and hailed until recently as a triumph of the open single market, the EU is abandoning market dynamics for regulation: gender quotas, mandatory transparency for pay equality, rules for platform work, a regulation for whistleblowers, even the symbolism of a

European minimum wage – and all in a few years.[34] This is legislating at the speed of light, compared to the EU's normal standards.

• In relation to climate policy, the EU has shifted from a technology-neutral, market-driven combination of emission standards and price incentives to a combination of central planning and technology steering, with a focus on European and national subsidized projects, under the well-known 'Green Deal' and 'Fit for 55' programmes that were recently complemented by political planning for net-zero technologies selected as strategic industries. Instead of enabling market forces and consumers, the EU is increasingly prescribing the what and the how for producers in the market.

• Regarding tax policy, the EU is shifting from being a platform for healthy international competition to becoming a kind of tax cartel, leveraging the size and power of the European internal market for the European coordination of national taxes. Through the EU, European countries unite in adopting minimum corporate taxes for multinationals, with or without international coordination from the Organisation for Economic Co-operation and Development (OECD).[35] The EU is also coordinating the implementation by all member states of temporary national taxes – a 'solidarity contribution' of at least 33 per cent – on any windfall profits that energy companies make as a result of the energy crisis following the Russian invasion of Ukraine.[36] It also seems inevitable that the EU will pursue an international coalition for import taxes based on greenhouse gas emissions, if only so as not to price its own European market out of the global market through unilateral European import taxes when it introduces its aforementioned CBAM.

• In the energy market and in the context of the de facto energy war with Russia, the EU is organizing an energy platform for, among other things, the European cooperative purchase of gas and a European price cap – in each case fundamentally reversing the market logic that the EU had previously maintained.[37] Changing geopolitical realities have ruined any ambition for a real energy market in Europe as market prices have become politically unbearable for member states.[38] Even for the pricing of (Covid) drugs, the European Commission is redrawing European political boundaries as part of a broad pharmaceutical strategy that seeks to subject the entire sector to European political ends.[39]

None of this is black and white, of course. It is not that the open single market is dead and buried. It is not that international trade is over. After all, the EU's historical mission and position as a haven of free trade remain evidently rooted in its basic treaty; precisely generating the challenge of legitimacy for the new power union that is eroding them, as we will see in chapter 5. And it is not that the EU has ever been a story of so-called market fundamentalism. On the contrary, more than half of all EU spending today remains linked to old-school subsidies and public projects: agricultural policy, European structural and investment funds, and European cohesion policy.[40]

European money for farmers, for long-term investments and for regional development of disadvantaged areas, in exchange for a free European market with open competition: that was always the deal for EU member states. It is the market piece that is unravelling. Since the Treaty of Lisbon (2007), the EU has formally stood for 'a highly competitive social market economy, aiming at full employment and social progress, and a high level of protection and improvement of the quality of the environment'.[41] The market in Europe is heavily balanced and conditioned, both by the member states and by the EU itself. However, the EU's current revolution is going one step further: it is instrumentalizing the European market for non-market purposes and subordinating it to them. In the revamped EU, the free internal market is no longer an end in itself; rather, it is a conditional means to achieve geopolitical, strategic, climatic, ecological and technological priorities.[42] As a result, the EU internal market has become less open, less internal and, well, less of a market.

I also make no judgement on the finality or the expediency of the examples given. To a large extent they, too, are a European response to an external reality that is mostly beyond the EU's control, especially regarding the intensification of economic nationalism by both the USA and China, against the backdrop of geopolitical conflict. Moreover, European coordination in this context is often preferable to chaotic competition among the member states. I mention these examples mainly to illustrate the change of tone in EU policy. The new EU seems to be seeking its new soft power through regulating and restricting the market rather than through maintaining an open single market, using the size and power of the European market to set international regulatory precedents.[43] Europe is profiling itself as a first mover, an international standard-setter, courtesy of its economic weight; this is yet another illustration of how the EU is abandoning the spirit of globalization that made it what it is.

This change of tone is affecting even the beating heart of European internal market policy, namely the practice of competition law with which the European Commission is supposed to enforce the separation of market from state and to protect free competition in Europe. While state intervention in the economy is growing hand over fist across Europe and record amounts of state subsidies are being recorded, state sanctioning is in decline. The European Commission is far less likely nowadays to prosecute any state for violating the principles of the free European single market; the number of such cases has fallen sharply.[44]

At the same time, there has been a dramatic rise in the state aid budgets the European Commission has formally approved, even since the end of the pandemic; this has been driven mainly by the war in Ukraine and by climate policy. According to the latest figures reported at the time of writing, the total amount of state aid being provided by member states in 2021 stood at €334 billion, which was more than three times the pre-pandemic levels; the European Commission has approved more than €730 billion in state support since March 2022 alone.[45] The European bureaucracy tasked with monitoring and enforcing fair competition in Europe's open single market apparently has priorities elsewhere that are absorbing its energy. Indeed, state aid in Europe is now no longer banned but organized, be it selectively and politically in strategic sectors,[46] or tacitly and stealthily through tolerance.

The basic yardstick of European competition law is also evolving, again signalling a new balance between governments and markets. In the past, the prosperity and the welfare of the individual consumer were the central concerns when judging market behaviour such as mergers, acquisitions or commercial agreements between companies. Competition law primarily served to foster low prices and high quality of products and services, to the exclusion of other legitimate motives, illustrating the separation that existed between markets and politics. Now, regulating competition in the European market also requires accommodating political considerations such as equality, consumer protection, social protection, public health, the environment, investment, transport and regional development. These flexible, collective objectives involve assessing market concentration from a political perspective rather than from a consumer welfare perspective, enabling more politically motivated market interference.[47] Take the climate crisis. If sustainability rather than price matters, then the paradigm of market regulation changes. In this scenario, the EU can accept corporate agreements and state aid that would previously have been rejected as anti-competitive and consumer-damaging. For example, a corporate cartel – a price agreement that normally would be anathema to the European single market – can then become a legal climate deal provided it allows companies to achieve their sustainability goals.[48] The borderline between markets and politics in the EU has become blurred, with the inevitable effect of enabling political activism by economic means.

State versus State

In the EU's metamorphosis, the internal market is now repurposed for a fundamental paradigm shift: as a lever for post-pandemic recovery politics and for industrial and climate policy on a European scale. Top-down planning and strategic coordination between government and business – in relation to climate, energy, technology, industry, sovereignty, resilience, security – are taking the place of the old single market that relied on the separation of government and business. Instrumentalizing the single market politically means instrumentalizing market players: corporations are becoming implementers of government plans or subcontractors of political authorities; consumer organizations are becoming public ministries responsible for enforcing political rights; competition authorities are becoming watchdogs guarding the political steering of the market; and so on.

This shift from market to state, from open market forces to politicization, from decentralized competition to central planning, from state abstention to state interference and activism, has fundamental implications both for the governance of the EU and for the EU member states. Through its single market, the EU was a platform for avoiding competition between countries and for organizing competition between firms. If the EU continues to trade the market for the state, it will become a platform for encouraging economic and financial competition between member countries, for reducing market competition between firms and for giving market status to those companies that are mobilized specifically as extensions of political agendas. An EU that prioritizes market forces is an EU that

stimulates a degree of common discipline and policy convergence among all its member states in one level playing field. An
EU that emphasizes state intervention over market discipline
is an EU that enables degrees of political divergence and pref-
erence in an uneven field.

A free internal market is compatible with the kind of diverse
democratic, political and governance culture that exists among
EU member states. The opposite means friction. Focusing on
industrial policy, government control and large-scale subsidy politics has the effect of organizing, financing and thus
exacerbating the differences in government operation and in
administrative and political cultures within the EU. Allocating
billions of EU money or accommodating billions in national
state aid for a battery factory or a chip factory in Germany, or
for a bridge between mainland Italy and the island of Sicily,
or for energy storage capacity in Hungary: these are completely different political realities for the EU to govern and
administer. Even with strings attached, EU subsidies inevitably
support incumbent national governments while reducing the
pressure for domestic reforms. Hungary's Viktor Orbán may
occasionally struggle to land EU funds, but he is clearly adept
at maximizing a financial return for his regime by playing the
bad cop in Brussels. A post-fascist Meloni government will
undoubtedly capitalize politically on the many billions in recovery funds Brussels is showering on Italy. The new EU is actively
mixing national differences in political culture, governance,
public procurement, corruption, corporate champions and the
like into European economic development. Sooner or later a
legitimacy crisis is bound to loom.

With a free internal market, the EU can serve all its member
states. In contrast, European industrial and climate policies
inevitably collide with the reality that the industrial and energy
interests differ greatly among member states, favouring or
disadvantaging some far more than others. Behind all strategic grant projects that are organized, financed, approved or

tolerated by the EU, there is inevitably a political reality of conflicting national interests, national and/or regional sensitivities and intra-European (im)balances; there is also likely a degree of political power play. The well-known teachings of the so-called Public Choice Theory, which looks at the economic consequences of political choice, as well as ample experience with state activism in our collective past should make us realize the political forces that inevitably become unleashed when governments enter into the business of planning, steering and subsidizing the economy.

A free internal market is compatible with power inequalities between large and small countries, and between richer and poorer countries. The reverse, again, means friction. Large-scale recovery and planning signal big budgets for big countries and big companies. State intervention in energy and climate means huge investment budgets in big and rich countries. The new EU is facilitating a European political-industrial complex in which the big member states and big business are necessarily at the forefront. The European post-Covid-19 recovery plan is targeted mainly towards Spain and Italy, allotting them €70 billion and €191 billion, respectively, out of the total pot of roughly €730 billion. Climate policy and crisis politics since the war in Ukraine have allowed Germany and France to bring out the big guns in state intervention and state aid, putting themselves in the front row for industrial and technological European innovation and rejuvenation. Of all the state aid authorized by the European Commission under the temporary crisis mechanism following the war in Ukraine, half has come from Germany: more than €90 billion since 2022.[49] No wonder Intel and TSMC are building chip-manufacturing mega-sites,[50] Tesla a giga-factory and Northvolt a mega-battery plant in Germany, all greased with billions in subsidies. No wonder perennially dirigiste and subsidy-bent France can roll out a veritable battery valley in northern France and entice big multinationals to 'Choose France'.[51]

A free internal market combined with shared fiscal discipline means a level playing field for all member states, facilitating gradual convergence in economic development. A fiscal union – like the aforementioned Stability and Growth Pact whose fiscal rules were suspended in the wake of the pandemic – reflects the equal treatment of all member states in macroeconomic policy, at least in principle if not always in practice. By contrast, budgetary flexibility and debt tolerance, the correlate of the tilt towards the state in Europe, mean an uneven playing field of divergence between member states. A debt union that accommodates and even facilitates sovereign debt creation through the strong eurozone is an EU of activist member states and governments that no longer act in European solidarity but instead behave nationally and nationalistically.

While the EU is set to restore a degree of normalcy in state spending rules in 2024, the new regime will remain more flexible, more gradual, more exception-prone and more tailored to the needs of individual states than before.[52] As a debt union, the EU is able to serve much less as a driver of common policy reforms that link economic to political integration; it becomes instead much more of a facilitator of national economic and political agendas. The bureaucratic practice of exercising European control over national budgets then means less European coordination of shared national fiscal responsibilities and more European special bilateral arrangements tailored to special or large member states. It is with the waning European fiscal standards as it is with the waxing European industrial policy: objectively they favour mainly large and/or strong countries.

A free internal market enables a clear political and institutional distribution of power between the EU, the member states and business. The reverse means friction. The EU is not a federal USA that can direct and invest from Brussels. An EU that organizes state intervention organizes either an arms race between member states or heavy bureaucracy for companies with European subsidy applications, or both. Statism in Europe means mostly complexity and fragmentation, in America mostly simplicity and centralization.[53] The EU is well suited to the technocratic oversight of a free internal market. But neither the EU nor any of its member states is capable of acting as a bureaucratic planner, steering the economy and coordinating large-scale industrial policy in concert with private companies. Indeed, what government – European or national – would have the capacity and the know-how to work strategically with multinationals and with large sectors without being led or captured by those industrial interests?

Its open internal market gives the EU a competitive advantage in terms of economic scale and political cohesion. Switching from market to state, on the other hand, means a competitive disadvantage for Europe: less scale and more fragmentation, less cohesion and more tension. The EU cannot beat the USA when it comes to combining entrepreneurship and industrial policy, and it cannot beat China in combining centralization with planning. These intrinsic limitations are threatening to saddle the EU with a loss of competitiveness and growth potential. An EU that increases climate and energy costs in Europe while reducing the level playing field of its internal market is an EU that will need to rely more and more on state action to compensate for its loss in competitiveness.

If economic growth in Europe disappoints, if competing regions gain international market share at the expense of Europe in the gigantic technological and energy transition of our time, the EU member states will lean even more towards intervention, nationalism and protectionism. The EU will then be either even more mobilized to selectively steer, subsidize and shield economic sectors in Europe, or even more threatened by internal competition among member states; in either case, the largest and richest member states will be the predictable winners.

5

The Crossroads

Is History Repeating Itself?

I have described the evolution of European integration and
the EU in relation to two fault lines: how do we want to deal
with each other inside Europe and how do we want to deal
with the world outside Europe? Beyond the loud noise and the
permanent excitement of politics and democracy, driven on by
successive waves of major crises, the answers to these eternal
European questions are fundamentally changing, and we are
beginning to glimpse the contours of a new EU.

We can see the history and the nature of European
unification, finalized in the form of the EU, in two phases. In
the first phase, the EU was a political response to the question
of how Europe wanted to organize itself in a world that, in
alliance with the USA during the Cold War or under globalization, was otherwise mostly Europe-friendly, especially
as the original threat from the Soviet Union gradually faded.
In the second phase, which is new but which is also ours,
the EU is becoming a geopolitical answer to the question of
how Europe wants to position itself in a world that, owing
to the great power rivalry between the USA and China as

well as to de-globalization, has become mostly Europe-unfriendly.

That tilt in global reality is existential for the EU project. Far more than any other region of the world, the EU is or was the consecration of a world order that is fundamentally over, even if some residue remains. As a result, Europe is economically, geopolitically and politically fragile, but at the same time the EU is strongly spurred to action. The EU undeniably has the wind of history in its sails. In what by European standards is the blink of an eye, the EU has undergone real transformation, a recasting in the facts of policy and politics that has taken shape mostly through successive actions amid successive crises, even if not quite yet in the political structures or in the minds of politicians and citizens. If it can continue to overcome political divisions, the EU will be ideally placed to take advantage of the revolution in our times to reinvent itself and thereby guarantee once again what has always been the ultimate goal of European unification: stronger, more prosperous and more secure European countries.

I have attempted to outline what the new direction is and where its final destination may lie. Above all, this is a fundamental question about the desirability of a proto-federal EU, about what is needed for a mature federal EU to function successfully, about what would constitute a workable institutional and political combination of centralization and decentralization in a Europe of states. How are we moving in that direction in Europe? Only à la Monnet, under the pressure of crisis, organically, pragmatically, technocratically, at summit meetings in Brussels or elsewhere? Or with national and European democratic leadership, with shared citizenship in an emerging European *demos*, with European solidarity? Through a united, collective effort involving the whole EU, or in a growing coalition of member countries that, as 'first movers' in a tiered EU, set the precedent and the template for other or newer member states? Do we want to move in that direction at all?

To answer that fundamental last question first, I suggest the parallel of history and the hypothesis of the alternative. In 1951–2, at the very beginning of what would subsequently become contemporary European unification, six pioneering European nation-states – Belgium, the Netherlands, Luxembourg, West Germany, France and Italy – attempted to incorporate their core industries (coal, steel and, later, nuclear power), their armies and their foreign policies into European communities. The pull of French national sovereignty caused the European Defence Community and the European Political Community to falter in the French parliament. But the motives and the methods of this aborted episode are recognizable. Europe's political fathers were still working in the shadow of war and under an acute threat from the communist Soviet Union under Stalin. They wanted to respond to that external threat with a unification that would pool economic, defence and political matters in European communities based on full-blown 'supra-national' or quasi-federal European powers. The impetus of Europe's external threat faded into cold-war stability under the aegis of the USA. And now many years later, in this twenty-first century, an external threat is back, but the US guarantee is partial and conditional at best. European alignment and autonomy are again necessary. European centralization and federalization seem inevitable again, once more with the mix of matters economic, defence and political. The future of the EU lies in its past.

For that matter, what would the alternative be? If the EU were not to become a geostrategic project, what would be our biotope on a continent with bloody external borders, great external demographic pressures, military and security risks, a front yard coveted by global rivals and a back yard played in by superpowers and rogue states? If the EU were not to become a superpower project, what would our clout be, what would be our ability to shape our own future and what would be the fate of our core European values in a world animated by superpower rivalry and by anti-Western revanchism in Russia, Asia and Africa?

If the response to Europe's new strategic reality is provided not partly through a proto-federal EU but instead through the panoply of European countries, what will be the strength or, on the contrary, the impotence of our continent, of our economies and societies? What could geopolitics in Europe mean without a European focus and bandwidth for the many national, emotional, religious, cultural, ethnic and geographical differences in the historical patchwork called Europe? How could we create safety and security in Europe without the EU as an anchor? In today's world disorder, where competing countries are all too eager to have a divided and à la carte Europe, what would be left of the original EU if 'every man [were] for himself' in Europe and every European country practised economic nationalism and protectionism? To take just one example, is it desirable or even feasible for each member state to strive separately for technological leadership, defence capacity and strategic autonomy? To ask these questions is to answer them. The new EU was born in the pandemonium of pandemic and war, out of the well-understood individual or shared self-interests of the member states themselves.[1] As a result, the future is more EU together, or more pandemonium apart.

An EU Trilemma

We must, however, keep in mind one fact: that the direction which seems inevitable by no means makes the progress obvious. Geostrategy, hard power and state control – the three pillars of the new EU – are not necessarily compatible. The realization of a broad and geostrategic Europe implies a greater number and diversity of member states that collectively may hinder coherent European power politics because of their divergent interests and values. And, vice versa, the need for the EU to become a coherent power union may complicate its enlargement and geostrategic positioning. Geographically, the EU would benefit from a broad Eurasian spread that minimizes strategic grey zones. However, the wider the geography of the union, the more pan-European or Eurasian its footprint, the more diverse the palette of history, values and historical interests among its countries, and the more difficult European common geopolitics inevitably becomes.

The new EU will be a permanent balancing act between necessary scale and necessary decisiveness, a continuous search for the intersection where scale is serving decisiveness instead of hindering it. From this perspective, the more the EU expands geostrategically, the more important its eastern member states become. As the EU develops into a border union, its member states with abrasive external borders become more important: Southern Europe and the Balkans for immigration; Eastern Europe, Northern Europe and the Baltic states for security. As the EU becomes a power union, the importance of European countries that have historical relations with problematic neighbours on our external borders grows: think Poland, Austria, Hungary, Serbia and Ukraine, all in relation to Russia. How should the EU build a coherent European power policy on that kaleidoscope?

Turning the EU into a geostrategic union and a power union exponentially raises the stakes of political coordination among member states. In an EU where shared state interests are limited to an open market playing field with common values, relations between member states are different and much easier to unite than in an EU that has to pursue hard (geo)political interests as a power bloc. Individual state interests will not spontaneously converge when it comes to power (geo)politics. The interests of larger member states will outweigh the interests of smaller member states, while coalition-building among member states will draw deeper internal EU divisions when it serves political issues that transcend the limited stakes of trade and markets of the old EU.

If the EU's member states re-militarize as NATO countries without European coordination, the trend towards power politics will likely embolden national interests, national champions and national spending, instead of furthering the emergence of the EU as a federalizing power union with a common defence mission. Without a critical coalition of member states that are prepared to integrate military investments and capabilities at least partially and de facto at the European level, including through technological and industrial pooling, the inevitable trend towards power politics may weaken rather than strengthen the EU. It is NATO alone, with European countries in staggered battle order under US control, or it is NATO together with a group of European countries forming the nucleus of a European defence union. Both options are conceivable. The latter is politically the most difficult, but it is also necessary if we are to respond effectively to the historical fusion of geography, economics, technology and defence in our time. An EU that does not become a (de facto) defence union cannot remain a strong economic union, and vice versa.

The shifts towards a planned climate-neutral economy and towards industrial policy in Europe are also complicating political convergence among EU member states. Brussels is not Washington or Beijing. The EU cannot direct or centralize Europe: it must above all mobilize and stimulate its member states. In doing so, it inevitably enables climate policies and industrial policies that serve national priorities, including national subsidy races. European protectionism and subsidy policies thus indirectly increase the national political competition among EU member states. Subsidy budgets are by definition zero-sum: one country's or company's gain is another one's pain. Is it realistic to expect those same member states to simultaneously override their national interests for more European integration in geostrategy and power politics, when these have become inseparable from economics and technology?

Clear European coordination or targeted European centralization – think of precedents such as Airbus in civil air-craft construction or the European Space Agency (ESA) in space and satellite technology development – can help.[2] Economic planning can also be linked to transnational geostrategy, for instance in building European energy infrastructure and a European battery economy supply chain across preferential countries, or with the future reconstruction of Ukraine.

State control and geostrategy can even overlap through European strategic autonomy in predetermined economic and technological sectors. There the sweet spot for superpower Europe lies: where the implementation of the EU's climate agenda, along with its industrial and technological strategies, requires new geopolitical and trade relations that must guar-antee the security and the autonomy of Europe. There the EU can extend its natural starting position as the central strategic planner with the necessary international trade deals and in the supporting geopolitical strategy. The European bureau-cracy certainly does not lack voluntarism, as evidenced by the impressive list of international energy partnerships that the EU has collected in just a few years, mentioned in chapter 3. However, even here the EU is playing mainly a ground-breaking role, facilitating the action and the implementation that remain at member-state level. Without mature European coordination and integration, 'European strategic autonomy' risks becoming the superlative of an industrial policy that, in the end, puts larger member states – France in the lead – and big national corporate champions in pole position for mas-sive state support and a pan-European market. The current praxis of the EU as an economic statism project rather than a free-market project thus complicates its evolution into a geo-strategic and superpower project.

We should also not forget how much the EU's transformation is rubbing against the grain of its historic mission as the creator and the guardian of a unified free market in Europe. The hard power of geography, borders, geopolitics, and of ecological, industrial and climate planning does not sit well with the soft power of the open market and of free trade. It is striking how the missing pieces of the European single market – services, banking and monetary union, transport and infrastructure – have been stalled by the EU itself in favour of an interventionist model with a domino effect of government interference at member-state level, objectively favouring larger or richer member states, and all facilitated by European debt policy. This shift is paradoxical because a mature European single market would produce the economies of scale and the European business champions necessary to fill the drive for more European strategic autonomy.

Except that markets work to the rhythm of business decisions and consumer preferences, not political planning. That the EU prioritizes the latter over the former says a lot: about the zeitgeist turning away from markets globally, about the underlying agendas of key EU member states, and about the loss of self-discipline in the separation of the market from the state in the EU. We witness within the EU the same spiral that feeds de-globalization worldwide: once a major country puts politics above the market, with degrees of interventionism, nationalism and protectionism, others must follow suit and everyone ends up pushing each other further into the same political logic and direction. Hence, the pendulum swing from the market to the state in Europe is affecting not only the relationships between the EU and its member states but also the relationships among the member states. This is eroding the political cohesion and the mutual trust that are the oil in the engine of the EU.

The three axes of EU transformation – geostrategy, power politics and state capitalism – are each in their own way changing the social contract between the EU and its member states and among the member states, as well as the European political weight of member states that are geographically, geopolitically or economically special. Aligning European geography, geopolitics and economics within a politically workable and stable EU will become the holy grail of European statesmanship in the coming years. The combination is theoretically conceivable, but daunting in practice: internal tensions are rife, among the three new pillars themselves and between those pillars and the foundations of the already existing EU, in particular its open single market.

The EU faces a trilemma: its metamorphosis, its existing political-institutional architecture and its European single market are almost impossible to combine. As a power union, the EU is eating away at its interstate balance and displacing the single market. While it may be unavoidable in times of need, when necessity trumps law, this can only prove to be contentious and eventually come back to haunt the project of European integration. The new EU thus faces a challenge of legitimacy.

Tension versus Legitimacy

The internal contradictions that could undermine the legitimacy of the new EU are not limited to the balance between state and market, and between member states. The EU is both historically and constitutionally a union of values based on human rights, democracy and the rule of law.[3] An EU tilting towards becoming a geopolitical power union is one where interests can conflict with and even supersede values.

We have learnt the hard way that democratic rule-of-law values are not naturally universal and that non-Western countries may claim legitimacy from non-Western identity: from the mix of history, religion and tradition in an alternative societal model. This is the reality that is penetrating the EU as it moves geostrategically in a Eurasian direction, and it is confronting the EU with a dilemma. Should the EU choose interests at the expense of values (example: Hungary is a member state), or values at the expense of interests (example: Turkey is not a member state)? It is a choice that the EU, on the one hand, can no longer evade but, on the other hand, must not make if it wants to be a geopolitical union. As a power union, the EU must avoid letting its values block its interests in its geostrategic Eurasian drive. Not a principled dilemma but a field of tension requiring a pragmatic balance.

Look at the realistic need for a border union. Here the tension between the open community of values and markets – the old EU – and the new EU is evident. The recent political agreement on migration policy shows an EU reluctantly able to soften an unworkable ideal of values – human rights, open borders and solidarity – in a delicate balance with a new reality of interests, borders and power. But it is a balance, a compromise susceptible to legitimate humanitarian criticism of its principles as well as its implementation. Such compromise should not prevent us from noting that the EU, through its transformation, is entering uncharted territory in which it is tinkering with its own principles. It will take steady hands and talented politicians to keep the EU on course.

According to its basic treaty, the EU is a limited supranational construction with enumerated powers, where sovereignty resides in principle with the member states and where political decisions remain as close as possible to the citizens, being at the level of the member states and not the EU.[4] So how far does this constitutional limitation stand from the de facto proto-federal state that the new EU undeniably constitutes? Of course, the transformation of the EU is the result of consensus or qualified majorities among member states freely transferring more sovereignty and power to the union. But that transfer is the cumulative result of crisis measures, not a recalibration of the EU's constitutional set-up towards federalism. Again, a fundamental legitimacy question arises. Without an adjusted quasi-federal framework, the quasi-federal reality of the EU clashes with democratic national sovereignty.

The clash between the transformed EU and democracy becomes head-on in light of the EU's pre-existing and well-known 'democratic deficit'. Of course, the EU is founded on democratic member states and its decision-making contains democratic elements, not least through the European Parliament.[5] But no one disputes that the functioning of the EU lacks democratic transparency and accountability, and that the EU fundamentally runs on a combination of bureaucratic technocracy and elite politics among diplomats and heads of government.[6] In the face of the EU's transformation, its democratic deficit is gradually becoming unbearable. The fact that geopolitics, border policy, international relations, defence, security, public health, industrial policy and technology strategy in Europe are increasingly in the hands of the EU, that the administration of the European Commission sets the tone and acts as planner-in-chief, that the EU often operates in a vacuum of democratic impotence or division at the national level, and that the EU, in its mission and policies, is becoming the mirror image of a USA that does rely on constitutional-democratic federalism: all this is increasingly problematic. As the EU grows in proto-federal stature and power, the democratic deficit that was intrinsic to the old EU becomes inimical to the legitimacy of the new EU.

The EU is quietly and gradually entering a stalemate with itself; the EU which puts democracy and the rule of law first is itself quietly and gradually drifting away from democracy and the rule of law. An EU that distances itself from its fundamental democratic values is essentially threatening itself. Under the old EU, the market was the overall compass and the democratic deficit was an operational flaw. In the new EU, there is no compass and the democratic deficit flaw is becoming systemic.

It is not just a question of whether the institutional and political mechanisms of the EU contain sufficient democratic elements, although that question is clearly becoming more pressing and more important. It is more a question of whether an EU that is leaning towards federalism can find grounding and legitimacy in what constitutes the democratic foundation of federalism everywhere: division between state and federal powers, separation of state powers and linked political decision-making power and democracy, at European level and between the EU and its member states, with constitutional guarantees. It is also more a question of how a democratic EU should evolve institutionally to accommodate a growing diversity of member states while executing its increasingly diverse political powers. It is also more a question of whether and how executive power within the new EU should be retained in a European Commission that was configured as a technocratic bureaucracy in a previous era but that has effectively become the hub of the EU as an emerging superpower.

None of these questions is easy to answer. Political decisions among European member states follow old and demanding rules for qualified majorities or unanimity. Given the inflation of new European priorities and the pace of the EU's transition, democratic political power at union level is necessarily limited to broad objectives or to ad hoc compromises. Either political power lies too much with the European bureaucracy or the EU lacks political force. Neither position is sustainable. Both can be temporarily displaced when a crisis forces emergency policies, such as with the pandemic, the Ukraine war and the energy shock, or as under the euro crisis. Both will worsen as the EU diversifies even further in member states and priorities, and as the state of crisis normalizes in a new reality.

The systemic democratic deficit, therefore, undermines not only the legitimacy but also the workability of the new

EU. It is at once an issue of constitutional-democratic rep-
resentation, of EU institutional design and of member state
engagement within the union. It erodes both the democratic
connection with the EU at member-state level – just look
at the rise of Eurosceptic political parties – and the political capabilities of the EU itself. Moreover, the EU's current
operating resources and its funding model are by no means
sufficient for the immense task of running a geographically
extensive and geopolitical border and power union. Besides
the inevitable politics of budget cycles, the facts are that
the overall EU budget remains a tiny fraction of the overall public expenditure of its member states, that its size and
composition have not evolved to mirror the rapid transformation of the EU's mission and that individual member
state contributions still constitute its lion's share. The simple
fact that the EU should now have its borders protected by
countries like Turkey or Tunisia already speaks volumes.
The EU is promising membership to Ukraine but lacks
the financial muscle to absorb Ukraine without drastically
reconfiguring its financial flows: that promise will return
like a boomerang, as it did with candidate country Turkey
before.

The EU's current decision-making apparatus, especially the
European civil service, is not equipped to deal with the panoply
of essential member state powers that have partially drifted to
Brussels through the EU's transformation. This is contributing
to the tension the new EU is generating between member states,
between economic sectors and between companies. The current procedures and instruments for implementing European
policies are also too cumbersome and too complex to compete
strategically with other power blocs. Europe cannot enter, let
alone win, a subsidy race with the USA or China, even though
it is now effectively being tasked to do so. The new EU risks
getting bogged down in the tension between its mission and
its capability.

We are experiencing the limits of Jean Monnet's wisdom in Europe. The EU that has always propelled itself forward organically and through crises is reaching its ceiling. A geo-strategic EU that is growing in territorial scope, in strategic geopolitical mission and in directing the European economy and member states alike is one that is facing major challenges if it is to remain a working union. For decades, the political capacity of the EU has been based on the entente between the main member states, the docility of other, usually smaller member states and the generosity of the richest member states. That formula is already under pressure and will only get more strained. There are limits to adding new layers to old structures. The EU was not conceived to be the energy union, the health union, the technology union, the geopolitical union, the border union or the power union that it is gradually and organically becoming.

And the EU's ability to move forward through ad hoc compromises should not distract us from the profound realization that a transformed EU faces a challenge of legitimacy at several levels: in its essential identity and position in the world order, in the balance between national democracy and supranationalism in Europe, in the basic contract among EU member states and in the operations of EU decision-making itself. Values versus interests and power, relationships among member states, national sovereignty versus European federalism: these are always tension points, and this applies not only to the EU's new priorities but also to the repurposing of its old ones.

Trade, for instance, is the exclusive competence of an EU that was not made to coordinate trade agreements as the extension of geopolitics and hard power strategy. The EU must take up its new role as headquarters for international raw materials policy and energy diplomacy as a kind of geopolitical entrepreneur that is pragmatic, opportunistic and voluntaristic, and driven more by a sense of urgency than by a coordinated vision. The gap between that old EU and the new world is now being filled with crisis policies in which the big member states are often decisive. But that is not sustainable. If the EU, alongside and with NATO, becomes the forum for European power politics, then that union requires an appropriate architecture to prevent itself from organizing, perhaps inadvertently, what it is supposed to prevent, namely the dominance of large member states. Its silent revolution is placing the EU at the crossroads and pushing it towards an exit.

Conclusion: Europe's Choice

Things are moving fast in Europe. In just a few short years, the EU has metamorphosed from a union of community, values and market into a fledgling union of geography, power and state. This silent revolution, of course, is gradual and partial. The old and the new EU coexist and overlap. The member states have collectively and organically chosen to make the EU the centre of superpower politics in Europe. Like other great powers the EU is now being called upon to define its geography, dominate its borders, develop and coordinate its defence and technology, strategically plan its industry and technology, and make its economy sustainable, resilient and autonomous.

The chosen direction for the new EU is the result of emergency politics under the external pressure of the polycrisis of our time: geopolitical rivalry and conflict in a new cold war with China, the Russian invasion of Ukraine, the end of globalization, the climate crisis, the pandemic. It is an implicit, derivative and mostly reactive choice, not an explicit, principled or proactive one. It is fledgling, vulnerable to political disagreements, to member state nationalism, to policy overreach, to the changing context, to a new crisis that may yet unfold and surprise. I have often sketched the choice as a trend, as the logical extrapolation of what has already been decided. But the choice being made is also real, fundamental and structural. It is epochal. It is directional for the long term and it is setting European unification on a new course.

The driving forces behind the EU's transformation are neither ephemeral nor superficial. Geopolitical conflict with China may be with us for the rest of the century. Consolidating European security and stability in relation to Russia and anchoring Ukraine in Europe is likely to take decades. The target deadline for transitioning to an emissions-neutral continent is 2050, at the earliest; in terms of restoring biodiversity, 2030 is only an initial benchmark.

The old EU was built on three pillars: a settled cultural-historical past that determined its geography; post-ideological technocratic market liberalism that determined its economy; and liberal-democratic consensus that united its values and interests. Each of these pillars is gone. History has returned with a vengeance, a turning point for Europe and the rest of the world. Globalization and technocratic neoliberalism are over; ideology and statism are back. Liberal-democratic values are being contested, while previously underestimated or ignored national traditions and identity politics now threaten to separate values from interests, both inside and outside Europe.

Precedents have been set and a tipping point seems to have been reached. The new EU is a centripetal force that will require successive rounds of European coordination, planning, intervention and financing as the years go by. The spectacular elan of this new 'passage to Europe' on the wave of crisis should not blind us to the weakness of its foundations.[1] The EU's transformation is a rupture in the historical trajectory of European integration. The new EU taking shape before our eyes is returning to the failed federalization of Europe in the wake of the Second World War. This is a Europe that the European nation-states have never wanted, one that the

European people have never chosen and for which the existing EU was never configured.

It is stunning how the EU's internal revolution is being carried along exclusively by a stream of political compromise with an undercurrent of technocratic planning. This is testament to the EU's creative power, to the ability of national political leaders to find in the EU the de facto catharsis of European crisis, time and again. But it also shows how hard power and superpower politics in Europe had become a vacuum after decades of open borders and free markets, a no-man's-land with member states spontaneously preferring the EU now that the outside world has woken them up.

The new EU must be careful not to lose touch with itself, with its member states or with the people of Europe. Its emergence through the prism of crisis, necessary and desirable in the light of the challenges of this century, implies deep contradictions and tensions: between values and interests, between democracy and technocracy, between national sovereignty and European authority, between EU mission and EU operations, between market and state, and between member states themselves. The new EU faces deep questions of legitimacy that cannot remain forever buried and ignored under the urgency of crisis policy and management.

The EU is silently and unwittingly approaching its US moment: the moment when a formally confederal union that has de facto evolved into proto-federalism should consider the step towards *de jure* federalism in order to preserve its original ideals and to fulfil its new mission. Transforming a de facto proto-federal EU into a full-fledged federal EU would be the ideal way to answer the new EU's existential questions, to overcome its internal contradictions and to adapt both its functioning and its financing to its mission. Nevertheless, the chances that the EU member states will together create a moment of great constitutional and democratic federal unity seem very slim, even non-existent. National referendums on the EU tend to be national and European traumas. To amend the basic treaty to fit a federal EU would be to create a black hole that would suck up all of the political energy in Europe. No national leader wants to make superpower Europe the stake in national elections.

But the new EU cannot continue to avoid its own shadow. Events that require European power politics are also penetrating national politics – just look at the migration issue, at debt politics or at Russian aggression. The mission of the new EU is also much more political than before. The shared compass of globalization and free markets has been exchanged for the open pragmatics of geopolitics and the indeterminate primacy of the state. Geopolitics, statism and politicization mean much more friction and interference between European and national politics. A successful European power union will also require additional capacity and resources, for instance for defence, security and critical industrial sectors. The current EU simply does not have the oxygen to integrate a country like Ukraine. In this, too, European and national politics will clash. If the EU does not become more democratic and transparent, at one point or another, one way or another, it risks confrontation with surprised voters who will be susceptible to demagogic anti-European populism. The lesson of Brexit should be borne firmly in mind.

Beyond the immediate urgency of crisis, the EU's transformation, its existing political-institutional architecture and its single market can hardly be sustainably combined. To break that trilemma, to avoid deadlock and conflict, national leaders will have to embrace the historic forces that are transforming the EU's mission in order to improve its institutional architecture as well. What cannot be achieved through a symbolic and democratic federal consecration of the EU could evolve through smaller, partial steps. Coalitions of member states deepening their political integration with a more layered and widened EU, using levers like defence, technology and infrastructure for precedents of pooling and federalization as first movers: this is the choice Europe has yet to make.

Such a choice would not be revolutionary; rather, it would be evolutionary, logical, even predictable, yet with something of a retro feel. Indeed, the Benelux union of Belgium, the Netherlands and Luxembourg is an eighty-year-old historical antecedent that still exists for this very purpose: to enable a cluster of EU member states to integrate earlier, faster and deeper than the rest of the EU.[2] In this too, the past points the way to the future of the EU. Recent inter-regional and multilateral initiatives on energy transition and infrastructure within Europe are modern bottom-up precedents for this: clusters and networks that de facto diversify, accelerate and deepen European integration, sometimes supported by companies and business sectors, sometimes by European neighbouring countries, often with the support of the European Commission, but essentially surpassing the institutional fabric of the EU itself.[3]

Europe has mastered the art of institutional creativity, of incremental progress and emerging coalitions. In 1985, in the idyllic border village of Schengen, France, Germany, Belgium, the Netherlands and Luxembourg decided to abolish their internal borders and harmonize their external borders. The Schengen Area now connects twenty-three EU member states and four non-member states in the largest area of free movement of people in the world.[4] Gradually expanding in parallel with the rest of the EU, even complementary beyond it, this is exactly the kind of thing that the new EU needs.

Then there is the monetary union. If a tiered and more federal EU in layers is the institutional key to anchoring the EU's role transformation, then the eurozone offers a striking example. A limited monetary union within the broader EU, a partial banking union, a separate fiscal union with its own mini-treaty,[5] the ECB as a lever for credit and solvency at European level: all of these are examples of how role renewal for the EU can trigger institutional innovation and diversification. It is all still imperfect and unfinished, but it proves once again that European institutional innovation can follow factual European integration. At the same time, the euro crisis has painfully taught us the risks of de facto European integration without a timely and adequate European institutional set-up; this is precisely the systemic risk for the new EU.

If the EU member states can find a way to match the EU's strategic momentum with an institutional momentum, the growing pains of the new EU could be cushioned and alleviated. The dynamics for this will be not only European but also international. Remember how the EU's transformation is a response to the external pressures of the changing world order. If the EU's strategic transformation is not appropriately anchored and supported institutionally in the union, it will render Europe strategically very vulnerable to external events, to internal divisions or simply to EU mission overload. Moreover, its new mission makes the EU the natural spearhead of Europe in the wider world. The EU must be able to answer Henry Kissinger's question – 'Who do I call if I want to speak to Europe?' – not only because the world requires it but also to serve its own European interests. The renewed EU will need to carry the torch for Europe in a changing world order that itself is entering a phase of renewal of international alliances, bodies and institutions. The international institutions created after the Second World War will gradually either evolve or be displaced in a new world where emerging powers are seeking recognition and where regional blocs are developing alternative institutions. In both scenarios, the EU is Europe's logical answer. The new multilateralism outside the EU will thus help renew the configuration of multilateralism within the EU towards European federalization.

Europeans may realize it too little and the rest of the world may barely see it, but a new superpower has already been born: that good old, dull, grey and elusive EU. There is still much to be named and determined in terms of choices, trade-offs, processes, modalities and so on. How do we construct a union in layers? How do the dynamics of European decision-making work in this next phase? How do we combine democratic legitimacy with institutional clout? How do we evolve towards a mature pyramid of revenue, expenditure and redistribution in the EU's public finances? How do we find the right balance between governments and markets, between national public debt and European fiscal rules? How do we position a transforming EU vis-à-vis countries and institutions, both inside and outside Europe and vice versa?

Owing to the strength of the polycrisis, Europe is the scene of major role-blurring amid great strategic role transformation: between the EU and NATO, between the EU and the Council of Europe or the Organization for Security and Cooperation in Europe, between the EU and the USA, between the EU and its member states, between large and smaller member states, between governments, markets and market players. If the revolution in the EU is to be successful, it must evolve towards a new transparency and balance in all these dimensions. The alternative is an organized country conflict within the EU itself, with great risks for all member states, especially the small ones, and ultimately for the entire European project itself.

Afterword: Five Beacons

The year 2024 is an important one for Europe – a year with European elections that will deliver a new European Parliament and a new European Commission; a year with US presidential elections in which support for the war in Europe will be a predictable theme; a year with Russian presidential elections, too. This is a great opportunity to make the EU's deep and rapid metamorphosis more politically visible, to bring it to the surface both democratically among European citizens and in the policy agendas of the renewed European institutions. Purely as an impetus for debate, I posit five broad beacons that could help consolidate the EU's transformation and provide initial answers to the internal tensions and legitimacy questions I have outlined.

1. Make EU membership multilayered and progressive

Having Ukraine as an EU candidate country is a unique opportunity to crystallize the EU's new geostrategic mission and growing diversity into gradations of membership that can be acquired more quickly, so as to anchor more countries in the union. Otherwise, Turkey-style agony risks threatening Ukraine and a rift beckons within the EU itself.

The way forward, therefore, is to redefine and reaffirm the components of EU membership according to the axes of the new EU, which are, crudely: geostrategy (security, defence, borders), geopolitics (trade, energy, international relations) and economics (market, climate, industry), on an indivisible base of values (democracy, rule of law, human rights). If we use that configuration for a progressive and partial membership in stages, axis by axis, it would shorten the duration of accession to the EU and leave the binary distinction between EU member states and third countries behind while maintaining, as much as possible, the coherence of partial membership by axis to avoid an 'à la carte' union.

Explore how a tiered membership could promote a path to faster or partial European integration for all candidate and other countries, including Turkey and the UK. That could be used as an alternative to the proliferation of preferential partnerships and alliances that the EU has developed with third countries over the decades. There is also a need to abandon the dogma that the European single market is one and indivisible. It should remain so for full EU membership, but access to the single market can be made partial and graduated, for example to avoid free migration where it is undesirable or unfeasible.

2. Build a defence union

All NATO member states in Europe are entering a period of rearmament. If the EU remains a bystander to this, Europe will miss a historic opportunity to connect its soft power with hard power in a world where one power is nothing without the other. At the same time, a European scale is the way to make the achievement of NATO goals by individual countries more fiscally realistic and to substantially improve both the efficiency and the effectiveness of military spending in Europe.

Supporting defence coordination at the EU level, at least for those member states that want it, however, requires a quartet of priorities. First is deeper European strategy around foreign policy across the spectrum of the military, industrial, technological and energy complex, in parallel and closely aligned with NATO strategy. Second is more European planning, streamlining and efficiency in investment and procurement, building on European cooperation initiatives that already exist. Third is focusing available European budgets more on the nucleus of a European defence union, which would also act as a financial incentive for member states to participate. Fourth and finally is taking the first steps towards creating a European army and a European command structure from among the participating countries. All of this would culminate in an EU that counts as a full-fledged pillar of NATO.

3. Strengthen the single market

An open single market is a crucial binder in an EU that is growing larger and more diverse, and in which the structural trend towards statism implies many internal tensions and legitimacy risks. The single market has come under pressure and is being undermined both by the EU itself and by the member states. The new EU should not undermine but rather strengthen the old union. With that in mind, I make some suggestions.

First and foremost is to develop a strategy for a deeper single market that answers the new era of de-globalization within Europe with more level playing field integration rather than more state intervention. The EU should not sideline but instead leverage its internal market to achieve its geopolitical, strategic and sustainability aims. A veritable capital markets union can liberate investment for a post-carbon economy. A

common defence market can fast-track rearmament without protectionism for national champions. An integrated
European energy grid infrastructure – cross-border electric-
ity, hydrogen, carbon capture and storage, negative emissions
and more – can support a post-carbon economy. A waste and
recycling market can enable a circular economy. And so on.

Second is to review and reaffirm European state aid rules
and end internal subsidy races between EU member states.
Third is to provide an emergency procedure for complaints
or vetting for market risks in European or national subsidies
and industrial policies, including distortion of competition and
protectionism, that is accessible to all stakeholders. To this
end, fourth is to consider establishing a European competition
authority to manage the tension between market and state
in the EU, thus ensuring that the European Commission no
longer oversees both.

Fifth is to focus European subsidies more on transnational
rather than on national needs. It makes much more sense to
subsidize the overall energy infrastructure that will enable all
emitters to reduce their emissions, instead of subsidizing individual countries or emitters, to give just one example. Relatedly,
sixth is to prioritize the technique of European projects in
which companies and countries from across the union can participate, rather than the technique of envelopes for individual
EU member states. And seventh is to make European subsidies
for member states more dependent on market reforms and
a return to fiscal orthodoxy in those member states, thereby
using European state capitalism to improve parallel market
capitalism and eurozone stability.

4. Increase European resources

The EU has been supercharged with important new missions,
but its overall budget remains stuck at barely more than 1 per

cent of the EU's gross domestic product (GDP). This cannot last. If the new EU is not given more financial resources and operational capabilities, it risks either collapsing under the weight of its new priorities or raising the importance of the big or deep-pocketed member countries to dangerously dominant levels. An EU that is serious about its de facto transformation cannot continue to improvise with budget items that scrape into multi-annual budgets. The EU's new strategic missions require a mature budgetary foundation that will also trigger a mature political debate on the direction of the union. Without it, the new EU will at best be a hyper-bureaucracy for countries and companies alike, at worst an enabler of all forms of protectionist state support at member-state level.

There are options. EU member states' contributions to the European budget could increase or change. The precedent of the European Recovery Fund – the creation of European debt or 'eurobonds' – that was set after the pandemic could be repeated for other purposes. The European banking system, with the backing of the EIB and within the contours of the ECB's monetary policy, could develop a financing vehicle with earmarked spending. A pan-European EU tax could be introduced.

I favour the last of these. The revamped EU is a proto-federal state that lacks contact with European citizens. A European 'federal' tax would tie an umbilical cord between the EU and national democracy. It would answer the need for resources in a way that also reduces the systemic democratic deficit of the new EU.

5. Institutionalize and democratize the new EU

The EU's strategic role change must be translated and anchored institutionally if the new EU is to respond to the internal contradictions and legitimacy risks raised by its merely de facto federalization. Institutional creativity drawn from the history of European unification offers tried-and-tested options. Specific European institutions or agencies can be given greater autonomy and clout for specific tasks; think of the ECB in monetary affairs or Frontex for guarding external borders. Also, groupings of EU member states can choose to integrate thematically within the broader EU further than other member states, even involving third countries, as through the Schengen Area for free movement of citizens. Clusters of EU member states can integrate deeper and further among themselves for their geographic region, alongside and complementary to the EU itself; think of the Benelux union or the Visegrád Group.

I also have some sympathy for the return of European communities, a dynamic that started in late 2022 with the creation of the European Political Community. European communities can reflect the main axes of the new EU – geostrategy, geopolitics and economics – including a European defence. Communities offer flexibility in involving countries in further European integration, both for third countries and for existing EU member states that prefer to wait for deeper integration into one community or another. They reduce the operational complexity involved in running a multilayered union. They also allow deepening the EU itself as the subset of member states that join all European communities in full, thereby making a smaller and more workable core for more European political integration.

One thing is clear. Care must be taken to ensure democratic transparency and decisiveness. The EU needs fewer top officials – fewer presidents and fewer commissioners in its Commission – with more democratic recognition as a result, more strategic, operational, governance and policy-making capacity, less complex decision-making, less decision by unanimity and more decision by majority. Whoever can combine this need with an intelligent institutional proto-federalization for the EU has my vote.

Notes

Introduction

1 Eurobarometer survey results often show a mix of positive European identity – in particular towards specific EU initiatives – and moderate levels of confidence or trust in the EU as an organization: https://europa.eu/eurobarometer/screen/home.

2 I thank Peter van Elsuwege, Hans De Wulf and Marc Maresceau (Ghent University), Stanislas Adam (Ghent University and Court of Justice of the European Union), Liesbet Van den Broeck (Ghent University and Federal Public Service Foreign Affairs), Sybe de Vries (Utrecht University), Simon Ghiotto (KULeuven), Gabriël Moens (The University of Queensland), Luc Rochtus (policy adviser, European Parliament), Didier Herbert (European Commission), Geert Bourgeois (Member of the European Parliament) and my good colleagues at the Itinera Institute (Brussels) for their suggestions and comments. All errors and opinions are mine.

Chapter 1

1 Along the same lines, following the Covid-19 pandemic, L. van Middelaar, *Pandemonium: Saving Europe*, Agenda, 2021.
2 See, e.g., C. Coker, *The Rise of the Civilizational State*, Polity, 2019.
3 See, e.g., the overviews on the Atlantic Council's *Global Sanctions Dashboard*: www.atlanticcouncil.org/programs/geoeconomics -center/global-sanctions-dashboard/.
4 O. Stuenkel, *The BRICS and the Future of Global Order*, Lexington Books, 2020; New York Times, 'Iran, Saudi Arabia and Egypt Invited to Join Emerging Nations Group', *New York Times*, 29 August 2023. Saudi Arabia, Iran, Argentina, Egypt, Ethiopia and the United Arab Emirates will join as of 2024.
5 This book was completed on 1 January 2024, at the start of a new year that sees an EU Presidency focused on strategic renewal (https://belgian-presidency.consilium.europa.eu/), followed by EU Elections.

Chapter 2

1 Articles 1–2 of the Treaty on European Union (TEU).
2 See in more detail the so-called Copenhagen criteria: https:// neighbourhood-enlargement.ec.europa.eu/enlargement-policy/ conditions-membership_en.
3 C. De Gruyter, *Beter wordt het niet. Een reis door het Habsburgse Rijk en de Europese Unie [It Doesn't Get Any Better: A Journey through the Habsburg Empire and the European Union]*, de Geus, 2022, p. 234.
4 Compare with H. Thompson, *Disorder: Hard Times in the 21st Century*, Oxford University Press, 2022.
5 Presidency Conclusions, Copenhagen, 12 and 13 December 2002, 15917/02: www.consilium.europa.eu/uedocs/cms_data/ docs/pressdata/en/ec/73774.pdf.

6 See R. Leppert, *How Exactly Do Countries Join the EU?*, Pew Research Center, 2022.

7 The idea of a graduated EU as a stepping stone to deepening EU integration with a hard core of member states has long been debated, even at the highest political level of the EU. See, e.g., Herman Van Rompuy, *Towards a Genuine Economic and Monetary Union*, Report of the President of the European Council, 2012: https://bit.ly/46SuCcL.

8 European Political Community Summit, 1 June 2023: https://epcsummit2023.md/.

9 See H. Kribbe, S. Lumet and L. van Middelaar, *Bringing the Greater European Family Together: New Perspectives on the European Political Community*, Brussels Institute for Geopolitics, 2023.

Chapter 3

1 F. Fukuyama, *The End of History and the Last Man*, Penguin, 2012.

2 See, e.g., G. Gerstle, *The Rise and Fall of the Neoliberal Order*, Oxford University Press, 2022.

3 The supposed intimate link between economic and political freedom was a foundation of the so-called neoliberalism that provided the intellectual basis for globalization. See, e.g., M. Friedman and R. Friedman, *Capitalism and Freedom*, University of Chicago Press, 1962; compare with B.M. Friedman, *The Moral Consequences of Economic Growth*, Knopf, 2005.

4 See, e.g., M. De Vos, *After the Meltdown: The Future of Capitalism and Globalization in the Age of the Twin Crises*, Shoehorn, 2010.

5 R. Cooper, *The Breaking of Nations: Order and Chaos in the Twenty-First Century*, Grove Press, 2003.

6 J. Rifkin, *The European Dream: How Europe's Vision of the Future Is Quietly Eclipsing the American Dream*, Penguin, 2004.

7 See, e.g., the World Value Survey: www.worldvaluessurvey .org/wvs.jsp; 'Thinking for themselves', *The Economist*, 12 August 2023.

8 See and compare, e.g., F. Fukuyama, *Identity*, Profile Books, 2018; J.-W. Müller, *What Is Populism?*, Penguin, 2016; G. Rachman, *The Age of the Strongman*, Other Press, 2022.

9 As predicted by R. Kaplan, *The Return of History and the End of Dreams*, Vintage, 2009.

10 See National Security Adviser Jake Sullivan's noted speech of 27 April 2023 on renewing US economic leadership: https:// bit.ly/3tvnnsS.

11 See, e.g., S. Jaishankar, *The India Way: Strategies for an Uncertain World*, HarperCollins, 2020.

12 See, e.g., U.S. Department of State, 'Summit for democracy 2023': www.state.gov/summit-for-democracy-2023/; Matthew Brown, 'How democratic are the countries at Biden's democracy summit?', *Washington Post*, 30 March 2023.

13 See, e.g., C. O'Brien, *Is US Industrial Policy Headed in the Wrong Direction?*, Lowy Institute, 16 June 2023.

14 See, e.g., B. Allan, J.I. Lewis and T. Oatley, 'Green industrial policy and the global transformation of climate politics', *Global Environmental Politics* (2021) 21(4): 1–19; A. Terzi, A. Singh and M. Sherwood, *Industrial Policy for the 21st Century: Lessons from the Past*, European Economy Discussion Paper 157, European Commission, 2022.

15 T. Friedman, *The World Is Flat: A Brief History of the 21st Century*, Farrar, Straus & Giroux, 2005.

16 See and compare, e.g., S. Aiyar, A. Ilyina, J. Chen et al., *Geoeconomic Fragmentation and the Future of Multilateralism*, Staff Discussion Note SDN/2023/001, IMF; P.K. Goldberg and T. Reed, *Is the Global Economy Deglobalizing? And If So, Why? And What Is Next?*, Working Paper 31115, NBER, 2023; 'The destructive new logic that threatens globalisation', *The Economist*, 12 January 2023.

17 See, e.g., É. Bassot, *The von der Leyen Commission's Priorities*

for 2019–2024, European Parliament, 2020: https://bit.ly/3M2lFFP.

18 See the European Council overview, 'EU sanctions against Russia explained': https://bit.ly/3RV7q9t.

19 See, e.g., M. Galeotti, *The Weaponisation of Everything: A Field Guide to the New Way of War*, Yale University Press, 2022.

20 EU, Foreign Direct Investment Screening Mechanism: https://eur-lex.europa.eu/eli/reg/2019/452/oj.

21 European Commission, *Factsheet – European Defence Fund*, 2021: https://bit.ly/3tyZvoh.

22 European Council, 'European Peace Facility': www.consilium.europa.eu/en/policies/european-peace-facility/.

23 European Council, 'European Peace Facility: Council agrees on second top-up of the overall financial ceiling by €3.5 billion', press release, 26 June 2023: https://bit.ly/48UojXN; see also European Commission, 'European Peace Facility': https://fpi.ec.europa.eu/what-we-do/european-peace-facility_en.

24 EU, Exports Control Regulation: https://eur-lex.europa.eu/eli/reg/2021/821.

25 EU–US Trade and Technology Council: https://bit.ly/478mc15.

26 See the EU Commission press release on the ACI, 'EU strengthens protection against economic coercion', 8 December 2021: https://bit.ly/3QjljNA.

27 European Commission, 'Updating the 2020 New Industrial Strategy: building a stronger single market for Europe's recovery', 5 May 2021: https://bit.ly/3tvuscJ.

28 European Commission, 'Global gateway': https://bit.ly/46Pew3p.

29 EIB Global, *Partnerships, People, Impact*, 2022: www.eib.org/attachments/lucalli/20220310_eib_global_flyer_en.pdf.

30 European Commission, Foreign Subsidies Regulation: https://bit.ly/48LIkjc.

31 European Commission, European Chips Act: https://bit.ly/3ZVf6KI.

32 See European Medicines Agency, 'A stronger role for EMA', 31 January 2022, on the EMA's role in crisis preparedness

and management of medicinal products and medical devices: www.ema.europa.eu/en/news/stronger-role-ema.

33 See European Commission, 'Defence: €500 million and new measures to urgently boost EU defence industry capacities in ammunition production', press release, 3 May 2023, on the Act in Support of Ammunition Production: https://ec.europa. eu/commission/presscorner/detail/en/ip_23_2569.

34 See the European Commission press release on the Single Market Emergency Instrument, 'Crisis-proofing the single market: equipping Europe with a robust toolbox to preserve free movement and availability of relevant goods and services', 19 September 2022: https://ec.europa.eu/commission/presscorner/detail/en/ IP_22_5443. At the time of writing, this instrument was still under political negotiation.

35 See M. Schuman, J. Fulton and T. Gering, *How Beijing's Newest Global Initiatives Seek to Remake the World Order*, Atlantic Council, Issue Brief, 2023.

36 Inter alia: Belt and Road, G20, BRICS and the Shanghai Cooperation Organisation. See A. Dreher, A. Fuchs and B. Parks, *Banking on Beijing: The Aims and Impacts of China's Overseas Development Program*, Cambridge University Press, 2022.

37 See the EU's Security, Defence and Crisis Response: 'The common security and defence policy', 12 August 2021, www.eeas.europa .eu/eeas/common-security-and-defence-policy_en.

38 J. Puglierin and J. Shapiro, *The Art of Vassalisation: How Russia's War on Ukraine Has Transformed Transatlantic Relations*, ECFR/489, 2023.

39 German Federal Government, *Strategy on China of the Government of the Federal Republic of Germany*, Federal Foreign Office, 2023: https://bit.ly/3POPF8U.

40 A. Brzozowski, 'EU proposes to recalibrate China strategy', *Euractiv*, 12 May 2023: https://bit.ly/3M6ymzd. The article discusses *Reshaping Our Relationship With China, Engaging With China, Competing With China* (2023), for now an unofficial document.

41 See and compare, e.g., M. Leonard, J. Pisani-Ferry, J. Shapiro, S. Tagliapietra and G. Wolff, *The Geopolitics of the Green Deal*, ECFR/371, 2021; C. Miller, *Chip War: The Fight for the World's Most Critical Technology*, Scribner, 2022.

42 See EU–Gulf Cooperation Council Clean Energy Partnership (2020); EU–China Energy Partnership (2021); EU–India Clean Energy Corridors Initiative (2021); EU–Japan Clean Energy Partnership (2021); EU–Israel Energy Partnership (2021); EU–Africa Energy Partnership Conference (2021); EU–Africa Clean Energy Corridors Initiative (2021); EU–Morocco Green Hydrogen Partnership (2022), EU–Tunisia Energy Partnership (2022); EU–Egypt Energy Partnership (2022); EU–South Korea Green Hydrogen Partnership (2022); EU–ASEAN [Association of Southeast Asian Nations] Energy Cooperation Strategy (2022); EU–Saudi Arabia Green Hydrogen Partnership (2022); EU–Vietnam Energy Partnership (2022); EU–Qatar Energy Dialogue (2022); EU–UAE Memorandum of Understanding on Energy Cooperation (2022); EU–Mongolia Energy Partnership (2023); EU–Indonesia Energy Partnership (2023); EU–Algeria Energy Dialogue (2023); EU–Nigeria Energy Partnership (2023); EU–Thailand Energy Partnership (2023); EU–South Africa Energy Partnership (2023); EU–Bahrain Energy Partnership (2023).

43 See, e.g., European Court of Auditors, *Audit Preview: Frontex*, 2020. It involves 3,000 staff and an annual budget of some €1.6 billion, a tenfold increase compared to 2015.

44 See A.-M. Sarantaki, *Frontex and the Rising of a New Border Control Culture in Europe*, Routledge, 2023.

45 See the European Council press release 'Migration policy: Council reaches agreement on key asylum and migration laws', 8 June 2023 https://bit.ly/3FfURhk, and the European Parliament press release 'Asylum and migration: Deal for more solidarity and responsibility sharing', 20 December 2023: https://bit.ly/3Heunhf.

Chapter 4

1 See, e.g., the Foreign Investment Risk Review Modernization Act (FIRRMA), the Committee on Foreign Investment in the United States (CFIUS), the ACI, the Creating Helpful Incentives to Produce Semiconductors (CHIPS) and Science Act, Build Back Better Supply Chains, the National Defense Authorization Act (NDAA), the Strategic National Stockpile, etc.

2 See, e.g., the Bipartisan Infrastructure Law, the CHIPS and Science Act, the Industrial Relations Act, the Foreign Direct Procurement Rule, the Entity List, CFIUS, as well as a series of presidential orders.

3 See, e.g., M. Cotta and P. Isernia (eds.), *The EU through Multiple Crises*, Routledge, 2021; M. Rooduijn, A.L.P. Pirro, D. Halikiopoulou et al., *The PopuList: An Overview of Populist, Far Right, Far Left and Eurosceptic Parties in Europe*, 2023: https://doi.org/10.17605/OSF.IO/2EWKQ.

4 See, e.g., T. Padoa-Schioppa, *The Road to Monetary Union in Europe*, Oxford University Press, 2001.

5 See, e.g., C. Barnard, *The Substantive Law of the EU: The Four Freedoms*, Oxford University Press, 2019; P. Craig and G. de Búrca, *EU Law: Text, Cases, and Materials*, Oxford University Press, 2020.

6 See, e.g., F. Amtenbrink, C. Herrmann and R. Repasi (eds.), *The EU Law of Economic and Monetary Union*, Oxford University Press, 2020; J. De Haan, S.C.W. Eijffinger and S. Waller, *The European Central Bank: Credibility, Transparency, and Centralization*, MIT Press, 2005; M. Sandbu, *Europe's Orphan: The Future of the Euro and the Politics of Debt*, Princeton University Press, 2017.

7 For a summary communication, see European Commission, *Happy Birthday: The Single Market Turns 30!*, January 2023: https://bit.ly/3FBZX81.

8 See European Council, 'European Green Deal': www.consilium.europa.eu/en/policies/green-deal/.

9   See EIB, 'Climate and environmental sustainability': www.eib.org /en/about/priorities/climate-action/index.

10 See ECB, 'Supporting the green transition': www.ecb.europa. eu/ecb/climate/green_transition/html/index.en.html.

11 See, e.g., N. Nugent and M. Rhinard, *European Commission*, Bloomsbury Academic, 2015.

12 European Commission, 'The European Green Deal: striving to be the first climate-neutral continent': https://climate.ec.europa. eu/eu-action/european-green-deal_en.

13 European Commission, 'Biodiversity Strategy for 2030': https:// environment.ec.europa.eu/strategy/biodiversity-strategy-2030 _en.

14 European Commission, 'Nature restoration law': https://bit.ly/ 3S1nu9M.

15 European Commission, 'Circular economy action plan': https:// bit.ly/3tEsdUp.

16 Compare with S. Cohen, W. Eimicke and A. Miller, *Sustainability Policy: Hastening the Transition to a Cleaner Economy*, Jossey-Bass, 2015.

17 See European Commission, 'European Industrial Strategy': https://bit.ly/3PUSrcR, and the May 2021 update: https://bit.ly/ 3tvuscJ.

18 European Commission, 'Important projects of common European interest (IPCEI)': https://bit.ly/3M0fwtD and 'Criteria for the analysis of the compatibility with the internal market of state aid to promote the execution of important projects of common European interest': https://bit.ly/3tT63hx.

19 European Commission, 'EU funding for climate action': https://climate.ec.europa.eu/eu-action/eu-funding-climate-action_en.

20 European Commission, 'An EU approach to enhance economic security', press release, 20 June 2023: https://bit.ly/3FiIQrq.

21 European Commission, 'Commission recommends carry-ing out risk assessments on four critical technology areas: advanced semiconductors, artificial intelligence, quantum,

biotechnologies', press release, 3 October 2023: https://ec.europa.eu/commission/presscorner/detail/en/ip_23_4735.

22 European Commission, 'Proposal for a regulation: European Critical Raw Materials Act': https://bit.ly/3ZU0nzR, and 'Critical raw materials: ensuring secure and sustainable supply chains for EU's green and digital future', press release, 16 March 2023: https://ec.europa.eu/commission/presscorner/detail/en/ip_23_1661.

23 European Commission, 'Proposal for a regulation: Net-Zero Industry Act': https://bit.ly/3tyfoLt, and 'The Net-Zero Industry Act: accelerating the transition to climate neutrality': https://bit.ly/48THUr6. For its adoption by the European Parliament, see https://bit.ly/3TVvIAZ.

24 Compare with the critique in S. Tagliapietra, R. Veugelers and J. Zettelmeyer, *Rebooting the European Union's Net-Zero Industry Act*, Bruegel, Policy Brief Issue 15/23, June 2023.

25 European Parliament, *EU Strategic Autonomy 2013–2023: From Concept to Capacity*, 8 July 2022: https://bit.ly/3Qhauv9; European Commission, 'Updating the 2020 New Industrial Strategy': https://bit.ly/3tvuscJ.

26 European Commission, 'The Recovery and Resilience Facility': https://bit.ly/3rPcb9X.

27 European Commission, *Factsheet – European Defence Fund*, 2021: https://bit.ly/3tyZvoh.

28 E. Dahlberg et al., *Legal Obstacles in Member States to Single Market Rules*, Publication for the committee on Internal Market and Consumer Protection, Policy Department for Economic, Scientific and Quality of Life Policies, European Parliament, 2020: https://bit.ly/3tAQjQc.

29 See, e.g., EU, Digital Markets Act: https://eur-lex.europa.eu/eli/reg/2022/1925.

30 EU, Corporate Sustainability Due Diligence Directive (proposal in the final stage of adoption): https://bit.ly/3tuB2jL.

31 EU, Deforestation Regulation: https://bit.ly/48RuBHL.

32 European Commission, Carbon Border Adjustment Mechanism: https://bit.ly/3PR9mx0.

33 European Commission, 'Joint EU–US statement on a global arrangement on sustainable steel and aluminium', press release, 31 October 2021: https://ec.europa.eu/commission/presscorner /detail/en/ip_21_5724.

34 In chronological order are the 2019 Whistleblower Protection Directive: https://bit.ly/3LZxa0o; the 2021 Platform Workers Directive (proposal): https://bit.ly/3M1hY32; the 2022 Adequate Minimum Wages Directive: https://bit.ly/3RW1tZX; the 2022 Directive on Improving the Gender Balance among Directors of Listed Companies and Related Measures: https://bit.ly/3S0cN7f; and the 2023 Pay Transparency Directive: https://www. consilium.europa.eu/en/policies/pay-transparency/.

35 EU, 2022 Minimum Tax Directive: https://bit.ly/3FiZcAh.

36 EU, Proposal for a Council regulation on an emergency intervention to address high energy prices, COM/2022/473final: https:// bit.ly/46wLXIh; C. Enache, *What European Countries Are Doing About Windfall Profit Taxes*, Tax Foundation, June 2023.

37 See the EU energy platform: https://energy.ec.europa.eu/topics /energy-security/eu-energy-platform_en; also see, on the Pricing Mechanism: 'Commission proposes a new EU instrument to limit excessive gas price spikes', press release, 22 November 2022:   https://ec.europa.eu/commission/presscorner/detail/en/ ip_22_7065.

38 European Commission, *REPowerEU: Joint European Action for More Affordable, Secure and Sustainable Energy*, COM(2022)108 final: https://bit.ly/3rUu2MM.

39 European Commission, 'Making medicines more affordable': https://bit.ly/3ZUIUXO.

40 See, e.g., the European Parliament summary 'The EU's expenditure': https://bit.ly/3ZYhn7P.

41 Article 3.3 TEU.

42 See, e.g., European Commission, *2023 Strategic Foresight Report: Sustainability and People's Wellbeing at the Heart of Europe's Open Strategic Autonomy*, COM(2023) 376 final: https://bit.ly /3Qhh8kb.

43 Compare with A. Bradford, *The Brussels Effect: How the European Union Rules the World*, Oxford University Press, 2020.

44 See European Commission reporting on 'Infringements': https://single-market-scoreboard.ec.europa.eu/enforcement-tools/infringements_en.

45 See, e.g., European Commission, 'Scoreboard': https://competition-policy.ec.europa.eu/state-aid/scoreboard_en, and 'State aid: 2022 Scoreboard shows that in 2021 state aid levels remained high to tackle economic effects of the pandemic', press release, 24 April 2023: https://ec.europa.eu/commission/presscorner/detail/en/ip_23_2407.

46 European Commission, 'A competition policy fit for new challenges': https://bit.ly/3FhQlPn.

47 See and compare, e.g., D. Bailey and L.E. John (eds.), *Bellamy & Child: European Union Law of Competition*, 8th edn, Oxford University Press, 2018; A. Ezrachi, *The Goals of EU Competition Law and the Digital Economy*, BEUC (Bureau Européen des Unions de Consommateurs [European Bureau of Consumer Unions]), 2018: https://bit.ly/3M1dh9k; European Parliament, 'Competition policy': www.europarl.europa.eu/factsheets/en/sheet/82/competition-policy.

48 See European Commission, 'Antitrust: Commission adopts new Horizontal Block Exemption Regulations and Horizontal Guidelines', press release, 1 June 2023: https://ec.europa.eu/commission/presscorner/detail/en/IP_23_2990.

49 Ian Johnston and Javier Espinoza, 'Ukraine war and green transition keep EU state aid near record level', *Financial Times*, 2 August 2023.

50 The initials TSMC stand for Taiwan Semiconductor Manufacturing Company.

51 See Choose France: www.elysee.fr/emmanuel-macron/choose-france.

52 See the Stability and Growth Pact: www.politico.eu/tag/stability-and-growth-pact/.

53 Compare J. Jansen, Ph. Jäger and N. Redeker, *For Climate, Profits, or Resilience? Why, Where and How the EU Should Respond to the Inflation Reduction Act*, Hertie School, Jacques Delors Centre, 2023.

Chapter 5

1 Compare with van Middelaar, *Pandemonium*.

2 The aforementioned IPCEI could evolve in this direction: a technique of bottom-up decentralized clustering that, through EU focus and funding, fills the needs of European centralization without top-down dirigisme.

3 All this is explicitly stated in the constitutional TEU and in the criteria that determine accession to the EU, the so-called Copenhagen criteria.

4 Article 5 TEU.

5 The European elections largely remain national elections with national parties. There is not yet a pan-European electoral politics that directly cultivates a pan-European *demos* through pan-European parties.

6 See, e.g., C. Bickerton, *The European Union: A Citizen's Guide*, Penguin, 2016; O. Costa and N. Brack, *How the EU Really Works*, Routledge, 2018.

Conclusion

1 L. van Middelaar, *The Passage to Europe: How a Continent Became a Union*, Yale University Press, 2013.

2 See https://www.benelux.int/nl/info-burgers/benelux-unie/

3 See, e.g., initiatives such as the North Sea Summit, the European Hydrogen Backbone, the Delta Corridor, the Pentalateral Energy Forum, or the Trilateral Chemical Region, as well as the diverse industrial alliances within the European

industrial strategy: https://single-market-economy.ec.europa.
eu/industry/strategy/industrial-alliances_en
4 See https://www.consilium.europa.eu/nl/policies/schengen-area/
5 The Treaty on Stability, Coordination and Governance in the
Economic and Monetary Union (2012).